A

Woman's Guide to True Contentment

A Biblical Study for Achieving Satisfaction in Life

Rhonda H. Kelley

New Hope® Publishers
Birmingham, Alabama

New Hope Publishers
P.O. Box 12065
Birmingham, AL 35202–2065

Scripture quotation on pages 69 and 71 are from the New American Standard Bible © 1973 by THE LOCKMAN FOUNDATION. All rights reserved.

All other Scripture quotations are from the NEW KING JAMES VERSION, © 1979, 1980, 1982, Thomas Nelson Inc. Publishers. All rights reserved. Used by permission.

All dictionary references are from Merriam Webster's Collegiate Dictionary, 1997.

Cover design by Pam Moore, Steve Diggs and Friends, Communications and Marketing.

Cover Photo: Peaches, Harold Sund, The Image Bank.

ISBN: 1-56309-433-9

A Woman's Guide to True Contentment

TABLE OF CONTENTS

Preface v

Introduction vi

Contentment Questionnaire—Pre-test vii

LESSON ONE   Acceptance with Satisfaction 1

LESSON TWO   Accepting Who God Is 9

LESSON THREE   Accepting Who You Are 17

LESSON FOUR   Accepting Your Spiritual Gifts 23

LESSON FIVE   Accepting Your Family 29

LESSON SIX   Accepting Your Finances 37

LESSON SEVEN   Accepting Your Circumstances 43

LESSON EIGHT   Accepting Your Life's Work 51

LESSON NINE   Avoiding Discontentment 57

LESSON TEN   Accepting Your Past 63

LESSON ELEVEN   Accepting Your Present 69

LESSON TWELVE   Accepting Your Future 75

Conclusion—Content in His Care 83

Contentment Questionnaire—Post-test 86

Group Teaching Guide 87

Bibliography 101

PREFACE

A recent women's magazine survey asked some probing questions: Are you satisfied with the life you are living? How would you change your life if you could? What is your heart's deepest desire? The world is concerned about personal satisfaction—contentment. Desiring happiness in life is human and natural. That desire for satisfaction seems greater today than ever before.

Christians also seek satisfaction in life. That human desire for contentment challenges the Christian's pursuit of God's will. I recently circulated a contentment questionnaire to several Christian friends. I asked them to rate their level of contentment and describe their pursuit of contentment. Although the majority reported a high level of contentment in life, they recognized factors that often cause discontentment—circumstances, poor health, fatigue, financial problems, stress, negative thoughts, and sin.

People in the world often depend on self, success, and situation for contentment. Therefore, their satisfaction in life can vary day by day and even minute by minute. Christians can have true contentment despite faltering self-esteem, limited success, or challenging situations. While personal contentment does not come easily or naturally, it is achievable for believers because of the faith relationship with Jesus Christ. Contentment for a believer is based on the Savior, not on self; on His sovereignty, not on personal success; on His supernatural power, not on a personal situation. To attain contentment, each believer must be committed to a growing relationship with the Lord.

I pray that God will use this biblical study of contentment to clarify your understanding of the sovereignty of God and to renew your resolve to depend on God for satisfaction and joy throughout your life. It is my prayer that God will give you true contentment expressed through a peace in your heart, a smile on your face, a lilt in your voice, and a bounce in your step. Genuine contentment despite circumstances ensures experiencing abundant blessings of God and is a powerful testimony of the Holy Spirit's work in a human life.

Join me and other Christian women in the lifelong journey to personal contentment, a journey that will lead you to total dependence on the Lord!

—*Rhonda Harrington Kelley*

INTRODUCTION

This 12-week Bible study is third in a series written especially for women. While there is no rigid sequence, each study is designed to guide Christian women in a personal study of God's Word. *A Woman's Guide to Spiritual Wellness* examines the book of Colossians and identifies biblical prescriptions for maintaining spiritual health. *A Woman's Guide to Personal Holiness* studies the Scriptures topically to affirm the holiness of God and to challenge Christian women to develop habits of holiness. This study, which follows a similar format, considers the subject of contentment—what it is, why it is important, and how it is achieved. Contentment is an issue of major concern to Christian women today.

A Woman's Guide to True Contentment contains 12 individual lessons to be studied personally and then shared with others. As you begin, examine your own heart. Are you satisfied? When are you discontent? Is your contentment contagious? How do you seek contentment? Complete the Contentment Questionnaire before you start the Bible study. Honestly facing your own thoughts and feelings is helpful. Retake the questionnaire after completing the Bible study to see how you have changed. While the questionnaire is a subjective guideline, it may help focus your heart and your head on things above.

Make a personal commitment to complete this study. It is easy to get busy or distracted, but you can develop spiritual strength to sustain you. A designated time and place can help you be more consistent. Gather some study tools—a preferred Bible translation, a pen and a highlighter, a dictionary, and Bible study resources. While the Holy Spirit will instruct you directly, He will also speak to you through other resources. This Bible study will use the New King James Version unless noted otherwise.

Each lesson in this Bible study will focus on one aspect of contentment. Scripture passages will be explored, explanations given, and application encouraged. As you read each lesson, look up the Scripture references and answer the questions. Bathe your study in prayer, seeking a personal word from the Lord. The lessons can be completed weekly over a 12-week period and should take about 30 to 45 minutes. Personalize the study to fit your own schedule!

A group teaching guide is included at the end of the book. If you utilize this study for a small group, encourage members to complete the lessons personally before group meetings. A group leader can organize the members and facilitate the discussion. Ideally, each weekly group meeting lasts for an hour. Group participation can multiply contentment.

As God gives you true contentment, spread the word. The world is seeking satisfaction, and you know where to find it! Encourage other Christians to depend on the Lord for satisfaction. Radiate the joy of the Lord to those who do not know Him. Point people to the Savior, the only Source of true contentment. May God bless your Bible study, and may this Bible study change your life and the lives of others!

CONTENTMENT QUESTIONNAIRE—PRE-TEST

1. I am content... _____ 1   2   3   4   5 _____

                         seldom if ever   sometimes   always

Why? _____

_____

_____

_____

Why not? _____

2. What do you understand contentment to be? _____

_____

3. What causes you to be content? _____

_____

4. What causes you to be discontent? _____

_____

5. How do you seek contentment? _____

_____

_____

6. Describe the contentment level of your spouse (if married). _____

_____

Comments: _____

_____

_____

_____

_____

"Now godliness with contentment is great gain" (1 Tim. 6:6).

CONTENTS FOR CONTENTMENT

The Bible teaches Christians how to live. The Old and New Testaments describe the godly or righteous life. Specific instructions are given to help believers know how to act, think, and feel. Christians are to be Christlike and to avoid sin. The Scripture is clear. However, the Bible also challenges the believer not simply to be godly but to be content in the godly life.

In 1 Timothy 6:6, the apostle Paul reminded young Timothy that *"godliness with contentment is much gain."* Paul, who spent much of his life and ministry in prison, was qualified to advise others to be content for he had learned to be content in whatever state or condition he found himself (Phil. 4:11). He knew personally the power of contentment in the life of a believer. Contentment added to godliness leads to abundant life.

Let's explore what is meant by contentment. What does God teach about contentment in His Word? What does the world seek for contentment? How do you find true contentment? As you begin this study, please develop your own definition of contentment.

Complete this sentence: Contentment is _____

_____

As you reflect on your own understanding, compare your definition to the world's perception of contentment.

What are the major differences between the world's view of contentment and a Christian's view? *World - Money, Job, Good Kids, health Christian - being happy with whatever God's will for you is* .
As you study the Bible, these differences may become clearer and more contradictory.

A dictionary defines contentment in several ways. In fact, the word must be defined first in part and then as a whole. The word *content* can be either an adjective or a verb, a description or an action. While the adjective *content* means *satisfied,* the verb *content* means *"to appease the desires of or limit one's requirements, desires, or actions."* Therefore, a person who is contented is satisfied with life, pleased with possessions, status, and situation.

Contentment is a noun meaning it *"the quality or state of being contented."* It is a person's condition reflected in spiritual, mental, and physical status. An individual's level of satisfaction affects every part of the being and results in either healthy or unhealthy, positive or negative, good or bad feelings.

In his book *The Road Most Traveled: Releasing the Power of Contentment in Your Life*, Robert Jeffress develops a helpful definition of contentment. His definition is based on the word *containment* from which *contentment* is derived. A person who is self-contained derives satisfaction from inner resources rather than external sources. He concludes that *contentment means being at peace with the unchangeable circumstances, choices, and even mistakes that shape our destiny* (Jeffress, pp. 28–29).

Because the Bible frequently uses the word *content,* let's examine this term from the biblical perspective. The *Holman Bible Dictionary* adds a condition to the secular definition of contentment. It is *"an internal satisfaction which does not demand changes in external circumstances"* (Trent, 1991). For the believer, contentment is not based on circumstances but is dependent on confidence in the Lord. Therefore, true contentment for the believer is acceptance with satisfaction—acceptance of life and its circumstances with complete joy and peace because God is in control. The believer's understanding of contentment is in stark contrast to the world's. Contentment for the world is based on self, while contentment for the believer is based on the Savior.

CONTENTMENT REQUIRES ACCEPTANCE

Do you really want to be content? Do you want to have that internal sense of satisfaction regardless of your circumstances? The first step toward contentment is acceptance. You must be willing to accept or receive the life that God has given you. Acceptance is a process that begins with an act of the will and continues to develop into sincere feelings of the heart.

What are some things in your life you must accept?

Many things in life must be accepted. In other words, some facts of life cannot be changed or altered and must be received or endured without argument. An individual must accept her nationality of origin, her birth history, her family heritage, her body type, and her basic temperament. These are some facts of life that a person must understand and accept. While attempts may be made to rise above these circumstances and improve the conditions, true contentment comes when a person chooses to accept these facts with satisfaction.

A Christian is also challenged to accept the consequences of personal choices. Let me share a personal example: I have come to accept my body type. I have a pear-shaped body. Over the years, I have come to realize that no matter how much I weigh, my weight always settles in my hips and thighs. Maybe you can identify! I have to admit that I still don't like the pear-shaped body type, but I have come to accept it as mine. There is nothing I can do to change it though I still must try to take care of my body. I have accepted my body as a creation of God, and I have developed a positive view of myself.

For the Christian, personal acceptance is a spiritual matter. We must be willing to receive from God His plan for our lives. We must believe that He always has our best interest in mind. The Bible teaches about acceptance. While it often uses the exact word *accept,* it frequently uses the word *believe.* Acceptance is recognition of truth or belief.

Read the following Scriptures and note what you learn about acceptance.
Leviticus 26:40–43 _____
Psalm 139:13–14 _____
Genesis 1:27 _____
Job 2:10 _____
Psalm 68:7–10 _____
1 Timothy 1:15–17 _____

John 3:16 is the foundational truth for all Christians. Belief in Jesus Christ and acceptance of Him as personal Savior bring salvation. Beyond that understanding, a Christian must accept other biblical truths. A believer must accept the consequences of her sin and the punishment that her guilt brings (Lev. 26:40–43). She needs to accept herself as a marvelous creation of God (Psalm 139:13–14), equal in the worth and value of all others (Gen. 1:27). She must accept the good and the bad circumstances of life (Job 2:10). A believer must accept God's provision and power (Psalm 68:7–10). Without sincere acceptance, there can be no contentment.

Paul the apostle came to an important realization recorded in 1 Timothy 1:15–17. The truth that he embraced was the only truth worthy of acceptance: "Christ Jesus came into the world to save sinners, of whom I am chief." Paul's acceptance of Christ as Savior was the basis for his personal contentment and brought glory to God. Your acceptance of God and His truths will make way for your own contentment and will bring glory to Christ your Lord.

Contentment does not imply passive thinking, lazy behavior, or apathetic feelings. In fact, contentment is the direct opposite. Contentment is acceptance with satisfaction which results in action. Specific actions demonstrate contentment to God, to self, and to the world. Without the evidence of godly actions, contentment could be questioned. Let's examine some of the actions that should result from a contented life.

Contented Christians are active Christians. They are not just busy do-ers but happy be-ers. Their internal contentment is reflected in their external behavior.

CONTENTMENT RESULTS IN ACTION

Read the following Scriptures and circle the verbs that indicate the desired actions of a contented Christian.

Mark 8:34 *"He said to them, 'Whoever desires to come after Me, let him deny himself, and take up his cross and follow Me.'"*

Matthew 11:29 *"Take My yoke upon you and learn from Me, for I am gentle and lowly in heart, and you will find rest for your souls."*

John 19:35 *"And he who has seen has testified, and his testimony is true; and he knows that he is telling the truth, so that you may believe."*

Galatians 5:13 *"You, brethren, have been called to liberty; . . . but through love serve one another."*

The first response of a contented Christian is to *follow* Jesus, not just in salvation but in life (Mark 8:34). Acceptance with satisfaction is possible because of the sovereignty of God, the knowledge that He is in control. God not only provides salvation but also offers guidance and assures power. Following Christ begins with the denial of selfish ambitions and the commitment to sacrificial living. Obedience is the key. To follow Christ, a believer obeys His teachings and seeks His will.

A second action of the contented Christian is to *learn* more about the Lord (Matt. 11:29). As a believer accepts the call of God to salvation and contentment, she desires to learn from the Lord about His nature, His work, and His will. Knowledge is not just the accumulation of facts. Knowledge is the confidence in who God is and how He works. Contentment, or acceptance with satisfaction, develops as the believer grows spiritually through Bible study and prayer. While contentment begins with acceptance, it must be continued with action. That action is obedience to follow the Lord and learn from Him.

Third, a Christian will express her contentment in her willingness to *testify*, to give God glory for the work in her life (John 19:35). A contented Christian is an outspoken Christian, one who cannot keep her joy to herself. A believer who knows the truth and has seen God work faithfully shares His message with others. Witnessing is a positive action that overflows from a life of contentment.

Another important action that results from contentment in our lives is *service*. The love of God produces contentment in our lives. The love of God through us can produce contentment in the lives of others. Paul challenged us to serve others through love: *"Through love serve one another"* (Gal. 5:13). Because of His love, we can be satisfied and find meaning in life. Because of His love, we can love others and minister to their needs. Ministry puts feet to a heart of contentment. When the Lord satisfies our souls, we want to serve others in His name.

Peter's mother-in-law is a glowing example of contentment resulting in service. When this godly woman became ill with a high fever, Jesus miraculously healed her. Three of the Gospels record this miracle that teaches about Jesus' sovereignty, servanthood, and humanity. The Gospel writers also teach us about the woman herself in these few verses. Each account clearly states her response—her action. She served. Immediately upon her healing, Peter's mother-in-law did what she did best, serving others (Matt. 8:14–15; Mark 1:29–31; Luke 4:38–39). The natural result of her contentment and joy was service. While God calls all of His children to accept His will with satisfaction, He also expects us to respond with action. Obedience, knowledge, witness, and ministry should be the response of contented Christians.

Contentment is a divine issue, a spiritual matter. It is not so much acquired or learned as it is infused or inspired. God Himself gives contentment to the believer who accepts with satisfaction both the Lord and life. Attitude reflects the indwelling of the Holy Spirit. A positive, godly attitude is obviously from the Lord, especially when facing challenging circumstances. That godly, positive attitude truly reflects contentment.

What kind of attitude do you have? Briefly describe your attitude toward the following people or things.

God _____
Family _____
Church _____
Work _____
Life _____

CONTENTMENT REFLECTS IN ATTITUDE

It may have been hard to describe your personal attitudes especially when you know how God *wants* you to feel about your life and its circumstances. He wants us to be content, to be positive, to be joyful. While God wants to *inspire* our attitudes, other people often *influence* our attitudes. The pressures of peers and the criticisms of others can influence our attitudes both positively and negatively.

I learned this lesson early in my professional career. While I have usually been a positive person and a contented Christian, my first job didn't provide an atmosphere of encouragement. I worked as a speech pathologist in a rehabilitation hospital. My colleagues were critical, negative, and judgmental. I never dreamed that their ungodly attitudes would affect me. In fact, I hoped that my Christian character would influence them. However, over time, I found myself becoming negative and harsh, condemning and sarcastic. I am grateful that one day God amplified my voice and mirrored my behavior to make me aware of the change in my spirit. I didn't like what I heard or saw. God restored to me the joy of my salvation. He helped me reclaim contentment, true acceptance with satisfaction. My personal contentment again radiated on my face, in my speech, and in my actions. If your attitude is not godly and gracious, you may need an attitude check.

Let's study the attitude of one person in the Bible to learn how God wants to reflect contentment.

Turn to the Old Testament passage of Ecclesiastes 1:1–11. Read the words of King Solomon. List below some words that describe his attitude.

_____

_____

_____

_____

_____

The words and tone of King Solomon clearly communicated his attitude toward life. He was bored, frustrated, hopeless, and disillusioned. Even the king of Jerusalem experienced discontentment. Neither his wealth nor power nor position satisfied him. His attitude was not only a negative influence on him but a discouraging message to his people. To Solomon, life was meaningless. He was discontent because he viewed life as a continuous treadmill going nowhere. He believed all human effort was useless and everyday life was monotonous. His monologue concluded without hope.

God began to work in the life of King Solomon, and he ultimately found satisfaction. Although Solomon faced trials, injustice, and anger, God changed Solomon's heart. His hopelessness was replaced with contentment as he saw God at work in his world. Read the conclusion of Solomon's story in Ecclesiastes 12:1–8.

Even though both soliloquies include the words _"vanity of vanities, all is vanity"_ (Eccl. 1:2; 12:8), the meaning of Solomon's words changed. God changed the messenger rather than the message. He changed Solomon's heart. God is capable of changing even the most contentious heart. In fact, only God can replace contention with contentment, strife with satisfaction.

As you read this final passage in Ecclesiastes, did you notice that King Solomon received answers to all of his tough life questions? Yes, bad things will happen to God's people (v. 1), and all people will grow old (v. 3); believers will face fears (v. 5), and everyone will experience physical death (v. 6). Without God, there is no meaning in life. Everything is in vain. But King Solomon learned what God wants all of His children to learn: God gives meaning to life. In Christ, there is contentment. Contentment changes a Christian's attitude.

Contentment is acceptance with satisfaction. Contentment requires acceptance, results in action, and reflects in attitude. While contentment does not come naturally to the human heart, the believer can be content because of the mercy of God. God can truly bring contentment to His children. Determine to be content. Develop this godly art.

Are you content with your life as it is right now? Why or why not?

_____

_____

What will you do to seek contentment?

_____

_____

"The Lord Himself is God in heaven above and on the earth beneath; there is no other" (Deut. 4:39).

CONTENTS FOR CONTENTMENT

Contentment in life involves accepting God for who He is. If you continue to expect God to be different or to respond differently, you will never be content. The secret of a contented life is confidence in God, both His character and His conduct. If you feel discontent, you may need to review what God reveals about Himself in the Bible.

Before we examine the Scripture, reflect on your own understanding of who God is.

Complete this sentence with a brief description or a list of adjectives to describe God. God is _____

_____

_____

Would your description of God clarify who God is for an unbeliever? Does your description of God confirm your own understanding of God? A clear understanding of God is necessary for contentment in the Christian life.

The Bible reveals all that we need to know about God. In reality, the Bible tells us more about God than we will ever be able to comprehend. As children of God growing in grace and knowledge, we are to understand more about God every day. Through faithful Bible study and daily obedience, Christians gain contentment in life because of who God is.

Who is God? The Bible says that there is one and only one God. The same God relates to His children in many ways. God is Creator (Gen. 1:1) and Redeemer (Isa. 63:16). He is King of kings and Lord of lords (Rev. 19:16). In addition, the Bible cites these attributes of God. God is eternal (Psalm 90), good (Psalm 119:68), faithful (Lam. 3:22–23), holy (Is. 6:3), just (Rom. 2:11), loving (1 John 4:7–11), patient (2 Peter 3:9), merciful (Eph. 2:4–9), and righteous (1 John 2:1). God is the source of grace (Eph 2:8–9) and truth (John 14:6). God reveals Himself to us as Father, Son, and Holy Spirit (John 14:7–18).

When a Christian is confident in who God is, contentment can result. Let's examine five of the most assuring attributes of God. These terms may be less familiar than others. Thus we need to have a clear understanding of them to insure our personal contentment and to inform others. Get out your Bible and your dictionary in order to better understand who God is. He is sovereign, omnipotent, omniscient, omnipresent, and immutable!

GOD IS SOVEREIGN

The Bible clearly teaches that God alone is sovereign. He is supreme in power, rank, authority, and work. Listen to the psalmist's proclamation of God's sovereignty in Psalm 113:4–6.

"The Lord is high above all nations,
His glory above the heavens.
Who is like the Lord our God,
Who dwells on high,
Who humbles Himself to behold
The things that are in the heavens and in the earth?"

There is no one like God. He is the supreme authority of the world.

As a child there were probably authorities in your life who earned your respect and your obedience. Maybe your authority was a parent, a principal, or a pastor. You sincerely considered that one a supreme authority, one with control over your life. While God does place people in our lives to have authority over us, He alone has authority over all the earth. He has authority over people, creatures, and things. God can use those in authority to teach us about the sovereignty of God.

Read the following Scriptures and fill in the blanks to describe God's sovereignty.

"Therefore know this day, and consider _____ in your heart, that the Lord Himself is _____ in _____ above and on the _____ beneath; there is no other" **(Deut. 4:39).**

"Before the mountains were brought forth, or ever You had formed the earth and the world, even from _____ to _____, You are God" **(Psalm 90:2).**

"You may know and believe Me, and understand that I am He. Before Me there was no God formed, nor shall there be after Me. ___, even ___, am the Lord, and besides Me there is no _____" **(Isa. 43:10b–11).**

"Oh, the depth of the riches both of the _____ and _____ of God! How unsearchable are His judgments and His ways past finding out!" **(Rom. 11:33).**

"He who is the blessed and only _____, the _____ of _____ and _____ of _____" (1 Tim. 6:15).

God alone is sovereign. He is ruler of heaven and earth (Deut. 4:39). He has been and always will be because He is everlasting (Psalm 90:2). He alone is God; there has been no other (Isa. 43:10–11). He is full of wisdom and knowledge and completely just in His judgments and ways (Rom. 11:33). God is the only one called Potentate, King of kings and Lord of lords (1 Tim. 6:15). These Scriptures can confirm for you that God is sovereign.

Christians often develop biblical jargon or a language called Christianese. It is easy for believers to use biblical terms spontaneously to discuss the work of God. While these words clearly communicate concepts to Christians, unbelievers may be totally confused. The omni-words are examples of Christianese, words understood only by mature Christians. There are three omni- words which describe the character and conduct of God. God is described as omnipotent, omniscient, and omnipresent! Let's consider each of these in our pursuit of contentment.

Do you know what Christians mean by the word *omnipotent*? If so, write your understanding here. Omnipotent means _____ _____.

GOD IS OMNIPOTENT

Omni- actually means *all* and *potent* means *powerful*. So omnipotent would logically mean *all powerful*. That is true about God. God is *omnipotent*. He is all powerful. He has unlimited power, sole authority, and eternal influence over heaven and earth.

God is the source of His own power. He actually spoke the world into existence (Psalm 33:9). His power is on display for all to see (Psalm 19:1–4). God's power is unequaled and will never be undone (Psalm 86:8–10; 93:2–4). He can do all things and strengthens His children to do all things (Phil 4:13).

Examine this key New Testament passage describing the power of God. Read 2 Corinthians 12:9 and rewrite the verse in your own words. _____

_____

_____

Were you able to capture the power of God with human words? Of course not. The power of God is beyond human understanding and human expression. However, Paul attempted to enlighten us with his statement of faith. God's power is sufficient for all our needs.

God uses His power for the good of His children, not to display His superiority. It is the power of God that provides salvation, transforms lives, conquers death, equips for service, and secures an eternal inheritance (Rom. 8:31–32). God's power provides, protects, and preserves His children.

It is the unlimited strength of an all-powerful God that works everything for good to those who have responded to His call (Rom. 8:28). The unlimited power of God is available to you, His child.

The New Testament concludes with the apostle John's vision of the Son of Man in His return to earth. In John's vision, all those created in heaven and earth were proclaiming the omnipotence of God. Together they shouted,

> *"Blessing and honor and glory and power*
> *Be to Him who sits on the throne,*
> *And to the Lamb, forever and ever"* (Rev. 5:13).

Their proclamation should forever be the cry of Christians. God is all powerful!

GOD IS OMNISCIENT

Another important attribute of God is His omniscience—the second of the *omni* words. What does omniscient mean? The dictionary actually defines this biblical term as infinite awareness, understanding, and insight (Merriam Webster, p. 811).

Now compare and contrast the omnipotence and omniscience of God. _____

_____
_____
_____

The subtle differences are important for Christians to understand. While *omnipotence* refers to the power of God, *omniscience* describes His knowledge. He is both all powerful and all knowing.

There are several key biblical passages that affirm the infinite knowledge of God.

Read the following Scriptures and draw a line to match each one with a truth about God's omniscience.

1 Corinthians 1:25	**God knows everything**
Matthew 6:8	**God knows good and evil**
Romans 8:29–30	**God knows our hearts**
Genesis 3:5	**God knows more than man**
2 Timothy 2:19	**God knows our needs**
Luke 16:15	**God knows His children**

God knows everything about every *thing*. He is totally aware of His creation. God knows everything about every *one*. He is completely attuned to the thoughts and feelings of His children. God knows at all times. He is continually in touch with the activities of His world. The most amazing realization is that the God who knows everything about us still chooses to love us.

Has it really dawned on you that God knows everything about you? That promise should be reassuring, but it is often nerve-wracking. I am often overwhelmed by the reality of God's omniscience. God knows me inside and out, my thoughts and my desires. He even knows what I think before I think it and what I do before I do it. (If you have forgotten this promise you may need to reread Psalm 139.) God who is all-knowing is also all-loving. The unconditional love of God added to the unlimited knowledge of God results in true contentment for the Christian. A God who knows all and cares for all produces contentment in all His children. His supernatural knowledge gives confidence to the Christian.

God's omniscience is something to be shared. He doesn't just store up His knowledge to become conceited or puffed up. God desires to share His knowledge with His children so that we can live life more abundantly. For the Christian, all knowledge should come from God. While we could learn from the world, we should choose to learn from God. Human knowledge is finite while God's knowledge is infinite. Like Jesus, we should grow in wisdom and knowledge as well as physical stature (Luke 2:52). Increased knowledge is accrued by the believer as we get to know God. The greatest challenge for a Christian is not to understand the knowledge of God but to know the mind of Christ, to have His attitude of love for all men (Phil. 2:5–11).

GOD IS OMNIPRESENT

The last of the three *omni-* words that describe God is *omnipresent*. He is all present. He exists everywhere. There is no place without God, and God is everywhere simultaneously. God is present in His creation and in His children. His presence convicts, comforts, conforms, and constrains Christians. The Holy Spirit reflects the universal presence of God in every believer, in many different ways, from the time of each one's personal conversion.

As a busy Christian woman, you would probably love to share this attribute of God. If only we could be omnipresent, everywhere at once. I often want to be several places at the same time, doing several things at once. For a human, this finite limitation is very frustrating. For God, His omnipresence insures His power. God is able to work in the lives of His children at all times because He is always with them. That is cause for contentment.

Let's examine an Old Testament passage describing the omnipresence of God as well as a New Testament passage.

Read Jeremiah 23:23–24 and then Acts 17:27–28. What truths do the two passages teach about God?

_____

_____

God is never far off. He is near at hand. He is always with you.

As a teenager I was both comforted and convicted by the omniscience of God. Knowing that God was fully aware of my every need was reassuring. However, accepting that He was constantly with me was somewhat threatening. My dad often chose the evening of an exciting date to remind me, "Jesus is with you everywhere you go." He clarified his message by saying, "Jesus is with you on that date, with that boy, and in that car." My dad's reminder of the omnipresence of God held me accountable for godly behavior. God's omnipresence is cause for contentment.

Are you grateful for the omnipresence of God? Or are you uncomfortable with His presence in all places at all times? List below the times and the places you feel comfortable when He is present or convicted when He is present.

Comfortable _____

_____

_____

_____

Convicted _____

_____

_____

_____

God's presence gives power to you, the believer who walks with Him. When you are alone, He is with you. When you are afraid, He is there to calm you. When you are weak, His presence gives you strength. When you are lost, He personally guides you. When you are tired, the ever-present God picks you up in His arms of love and carries you. You can never know the care of God without an understanding of the constant presence of God. Great contentment in life is possible because of the eternal existence of God in your life.

GOD IS IMMUTABLE

God is not only sovereign, omnipotent, omniscient, and omnipresent. He is also immutable or unchanging. He will never be more than what He is, nor will He ever be less. Nothing about God ever changes. The Lord Himself told the prophet Malachi, "For I am the Lord, I do not change" (Mal. 3:6). That is a great promise!

The world today is always changing. In fact, it has been said that the only inevitable in life is change. While most of us don't like change because we like our comfort zones, we come to accept change as a fact

14

of life. People change. Circumstances change. Change forces itself on us, but the Christians can find contentment in a God who never changes. Someone has said, "Change is inevitable except from a vending machine!" How true!

We need to understand three parts to the definition of *immutable* in terms of God's character: He does not change; He is not capable of change; He does not choose to change. Because He is God, He never changes His mind and never alters His plan. His plans, which are always perfect, remain the same. God who is unchanging in His basic nature never chooses to change. He is confident in His constancy. We can be, too.

Turn in your Bible to Psalm 102:24–28. After you read this Old Testament passage, read its cross-reference in the New Testament, Hebrews 1:10–12. Then answer these questions:
Who is unchanging? _____
Who is changing? _____

Even when the psalmist was afflicted, he confidently praised God's immutable character. God alone will endure when all else perishes. God will remain the same while all others change. God will live forever while everyone else dies. Believers can be sure of God. He who has never changed will never change.

God is the same yesterday, today, and forever. God is the same with all people of all generations. He is the same because His nature is immutable. Claim the unchanging character of God, and He will give you contentment.

As we conclude this study of who God is, identify the following statements as true or false by circling the T or F.

God is the only true God.	T or F	
God is our supreme authority.	T or F	
God has unlimited power.	T or F	
God has infinite knowledge.	T or F	
God is everywhere simultaneously.	T or F	
God is always the same.	T or F	

Each of the previous statements is true because God truly is sovereign, all powerful, all knowing, all present, and unchanging. While an understanding of who God is produces contentment in a believer, the full understanding of contentment is actually found in the word *is*: accepting who God is. Contentment comes from a God who relates to His children personally.

An unknown person expressed the importance of God's active involvement in our lives in this way:

"Describe him as you will: good, fair Lord, sweet, merciful, righteous, wise, all-knowing, strong one, almighty; as knowledge, wisdom, might, strength, love, or charity, and you will find them all hidden and contained in this little word *is*" (from *The Book of Privy Counseling* recorded in *The Wisdom of the Saints*, p. 8).

A Christian grows spiritually as she better understands the attributes of God. However, the attributes of God affect the Christian's life when she realizes the active involvement of the Lord in her life. God is interested in you; He cares for you; He provides for you; He strengthens you; He guides you. He is *your* God, not just the God of the universe. That is an important cause for contentment.

CUSTOMIZE CONTENTMENT

Who is God to you? _____

_____

How do the attributes of God affect your life? _____

_____

What can you do to claim the promises of God? _____

_____

"You are a chosen generation, a royal priest-hood, a holy nation, His own special people" (1 Pet. 2:9).

CONTENTS FOR CONTENTMENT

True contentment begins with acceptance of God for who He is and continues with acceptance of self. A Christian should have no trouble accepting God, but she often struggles in accepting herself. There is no real satisfaction in life without personal acceptance.

Christians throughout the centuries have struggled with these issues. Poor self worth and low self-esteem rob a Christian of joy and abundant life. Criticizing and demeaning one's self is so human. Even Moses, the great leader of the Israelites, felt insecure and unworthy. Though he led his people out of slavery through the wilderness and into the Promised Land, Moses never felt confident in Himself. He was, however, confident in God and content because of God's character.

The story of Moses' life is recorded in Exodus 1 through Deuteronomy 34. This Hebrew baby who was protected by his mother and raised as royalty by Pharaoh's daughter became a hero despite his own weaknesses. As a young man, Moses saw the sufferings of his people and fled Egypt to the land of Midian. There he worked for the priest of Midian and married one of his daughters. Even as a stranger in a foreign land, Moses was content.

Read Exodus 2:21–22 and fill in the blank in the following Scripture: "Moses was _____ to live with the man, and he gave Zipporah his daughter to Moses" (Ex. 2:21). Why do you think Moses was content? _____

_____

_____

Moses was satisfied with his life though his circumstances changed greatly. He was content because he was following the Lord.

Moses' experience at the burning bush was a spiritual turning point as he met God personally (Ex. 3:1–6). However, Moses doubted his own ability when God called him to return to his people with a divine message. He did not think he could speak well enough to be a spokesman for God (Ex. 4:10–12). While Moses questioned himself, the response focused on God. While God's children may doubt their own strength, they should not doubt the power of God.

In obedience to God, Moses returned to Egypt to free his people from slavery. He faithfully led them through the wilderness for 40 years, facing dangers and peril. God always protected Moses and the Israelites. He was not only a hero but a religious leader used by God to deliver the law (Ex. 20–23) and build the tabernacle (Ex. 26–28).

As spiritual leadership was established in the tabernacle, Moses again struggled with his own personal contentment. The conduct for priests had been prescribed by God, but the priests often abused their position of prominence and engaged in immoral behavior. Moses was content when they made a sin offering, seeking God's forgiveness.

Read Leviticus 10:20 and fill in the blank in this Scripture: "So when Moses heard that, he was _____." Why do you think Moses was content? _____ While Moses did not have confidence in himself or others, he had confidence in God. Thus, he was content.

Moses struggled with his self doubt and sinful nature throughout his life. Because of his own sin, God did not allow Moses to enter the Promised Land (Num. 20). At the time of his death, God was with Moses to comfort him. The life of Moses is a testimony to Christians today about dependence on God and not on self. God blessed Moses through their intimate relationship. Moses depicted for others confidence in God. Moses, who accepted God wholeheartedly, accepted himself and even his limitations. When Moses turned away from contentment and acceptance, he had problems. Now that we have examined the life of one Bible character, let's study a biblical teaching about who we are in Christ.

YOU ARE CHOSEN

The apostle Peter tried to answer the question *Who am I?* in his first New Testament epistle. He wanted to accept himself and encourage others to understand their value in Christ. His simple but profound explanation can help believers find true contentment in themselves.

As you read 1 Peter 2:9–10, underline any words that describe who you are.

If you believe what God's Word says about you, then you can be content, accepting yourself as God's chosen one.

Peter began his affirmation of self worth by focusing on God. You have been chosen by God. In Deuteronomy 14:2, Moses told the Hebrews: *"you are a holy people to the Lord your God, and the Lord has chosen you to be a people for Himself, a special treasure above all the peoples who are on the face of the earth."* God has chosen you. He has *chosen you* to be His child. God offers salvation. You must choose to accept it or reject it.

Have you responded to God's call to salvation? If so, write a brief personal testimony of your faith on a separate sheet of paper.

If you have not accepted God's gift of salvation, please know that you can be saved by asking Him to forgive your sin and by accepting Him as Savior. You can be saved right now because God has chosen you to be His child. You no longer have to depend on self. You can depend on God. That is cause for contentment.

Being chosen is important to most people, especially Christians. Whether it is being chosen for a sports team or for a high school date, the choice of another person to select you affirms personal worth and value. I remember well how excited I was as a child to be chosen as a team player or best friend. As a teenager, I was thrilled to be chosen as cheerleader or yearbook editor. As a young adult, I was grateful to be chosen by my husband to be his wife. And in 1996, I was overjoyed when my husband was chosen to be president of a seminary in New Orleans. As we serve the Lord together here, I am content not only with my life but what God has chosen for us to do. Contentment for a Christian is knowing that God has chosen you to be His child.

True contentment also comes from knowing that God has a purpose for you. You have been chosen, and God calls you *"a royal priesthood"* (1 Pet. 2:9). Not only are you royalty, you are a child of the King. You are a priest, one who has direct access to God without any mediator other than Christ. The Bible does not use the word *priesthood* to mean a position of power in the church. Instead, Scripture affirms your own personal relationship with God. You are His child by His act of grace and His priest by your access to Him. As His priest, you have a job to do.

Read Revelation 5:9–10. Then write that passage in your words in the margin.

The Scripture affirms your worth as royalty, an heir to all that is God's, and as a priest, a co-laborer with God in His work here on earth. Christians today can believe in the priesthood of the believer and therefore have cause for contentment. This doctrine affects your life in two ways. It strengthens your relationship with God, and it structures your relationship with others. A human priest is not necessary for a believer to relate directly to God. Every Christian has access personally to God through faith in Jesus Christ and the work of the Holy Spirit. God speaks directly to the believer through prayer and Bible study. As the writer said in Hebrews, *"Let us therefore come boldly to the throne of grace, that we may obtain mercy and find grace to help in the time of need"* (Heb. 4:16).

Christians are to commune with God intimately and are to minister to others in His name. The priesthood of the believer also includes an assignment to service. Every believer should share God's Word with others and minister His grace to them. The function of the priesthood which gives responsibility and meaningful ministry also strengthens self-worth.

YOU ARE ROYAL

Paul the apostle taught young Timothy about the Lord and ministry. He clarified doctrine and encouraged perseverance in the work of the Kingdom. He discussed leadership roles in the church and prescribed godly behavior. The apostle clearly instructed this child in the faith about his relationship with God and responsibility to serve. In 1 Timothy 2:5,7 Paul reminded Timothy, *"There is one God and one Mediator between God and men, the Man Christ Jesus, . . . for which I was appointed a preacher and an apostle."* As a believer, you are a priest relating directly to God and ministering personally to others. A priest is to share God's Word with others and minister in His name. God has that purpose for your life. Accomplishing God's purpose can lead to personal contentment.

YOU ARE HOLY

In 1 Peter 2:9–10, the apostle Peter described who you are as a believer. He said you are *chosen*, you are *royal*, and you are *holy*. As a believer you have been selected by God, created for a purpose, and set apart for righteousness. You are His child, and you should be holy. He is a holy God, and you are to be His holy child.

In the beginning, God created you in His image (Gen. 1:27). God by His very nature is set apart, without sin, evoking awe. Therefore, you were created in His image of holiness. The prophet Isaiah reminds us of the holiness of God: *"Holy, holy, holy is the Lord of hosts; the whole earth is full of His glory!"* (Isa. 6:3). God calls His children to holiness. *"As He who called you is holy, you also be holy in all your conduct, because it is written, 'Be holy, for I am holy'"* (1 Pet. 1:15–16).

A holy life brings glory to God and gives personal joy and peace. The Scripture assures us that godly living pleases God and one's self. If you are not pleased with yourself, you may be falling short of God's standard. Being holy does not mean being religious—it means being set apart for God's purposes. The blessings of holiness come immediately and eternally for those who are holy. Carefully read Romans 6:22: *"But now having been set free from sin, and having become slaves of God, you have your fruit to holiness, and the end, everlasting life."*

Are you holy? Are your thoughts and actions godly?

Rate your holiness on the scale below with 1 being the lowest and 5 being the highest. Circle a number which honestly reflects your character.

	unholy				holy
My thoughts are	1	2	3	4	5
My words are	1	2	3	4	5
My feelings are	1	2	3	4	5
My actions are	1	2	3	4	5

A careful evaluation of personal behavior is an essential step toward contentment. Ungodly behavior leads to discontentment and godly behavior results in contentment. If you believe you are a chosen generation and a royal priesthood, you cannot be satisfied with an unholy life. Those who are chosen and royal are also to be holy. Contentment only comes if you are the person God created you to be.

Remember, you can turn away from your unrighteous behavior and be forgiven if you confess your sin. First John 1:9 says: *"If we confess our sins, He is faithful and just to forgive us our sins and to cleanse us from all unrighteousness."* If you truly want to be happy, you must get your life right with God. Then He will pour out His blessings on you. One of His greatest blessings is personal contentment. (For a more indepth study of biblical holiness, I recommend *A Woman's Guide to Personal Holiness.*)

You Are Special

Peter concluded his description of your character by calling you special. Whether you feel like it or not, you are special. Whether you look like it or not, you are special. If you are a believer, God calls you special. You are His special person. We, as children of God, are His special people.

Special has always been one of my favorite words. If I am not careful, I overuse it. In writing a thank you note, I am tempted to express gratitude to a special friend for a special time and a special memory. I have often wondered what has drawn me to that word. Certainly, I like to feel special. I enjoy special times. And, I savor special memories. To be called "special" by God thrills me. I am His special child. We are His special people.

The dictionary definition of the word *special* helps me understand why I like the word so much. *Special* actually means *"being in some way superior; held in particular esteem; readily distinguishable from others"* (Merriam Webster, p. 1128). To God, you are special. Because you are His chosen child, a royal priesthood, a holy one, you are distinguishable from others. Those who are created by God and called to Him are surely special. We have been given the extraordinary task of introducing God to others.

What is special to you? List below some people and things that you consider to be special. Then briefly describe why they mean so much to you.

Who? _____

What? _____

_____

Why? _____

_____

These people and things are special to you because in your opinion they are superior to others, highly esteemed, or unlike all others.

In God's eyes you are special. You are special because He has chosen you for the purpose of being holy. You are special because you are:

- God's child;
- God's likeness;
- God's messenger;
- God's creation.

Though it is humanly impossible to fully understand this truth, you can find great contentment as you accept God's design for who you are. He affirms you as worthy.

Like Moses, you may feel inadequate or unworthy. As God did with Moses, He has chosen you to be His child. He wants you to fulfill His purpose and live a holy life. He wants you to know you are special in His eyes. Then, you will be able to *"proclaim the praises of Him"* (1 Pet. 2:9). The God who has called you out of darkness has called you into His marvelous light. Though you once were not His people, you are now. Though you once had no mercy, God has given you His mercy. God has created you in His image, made you His child, assigned you His task, and called you His special people. That is why believers should be content.

While the world may determine your worth by what you do, the Bible affirms your worth by who you are. You are chosen; you are royal; you are holy; you are special. That understanding should strengthen your self-worth. Your great value to God should be cause for contentment.

CUSTOMIZE CONTENTMENT

Fill in your name below to personilize this biblical teaching about your personhood in Jesus Christ.

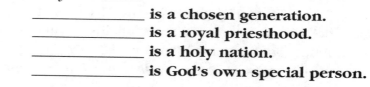

_____ **is a chosen generation.**
_____ **is a royal priesthood.**
_____ **is a holy nation.**
_____ **is God's own special person.**

Those biblical affirmations should strengthen your self-esteem and give you true contentment.

Now complete these sentences to recall who you are and what God desires.
I am a chosen _____.
I am a royal priesthood to _____.
I am holy in _____.
I am special because _____.

You can be content in who you are if you are confident in who God is.

"As each one has received a gift, minister it to one another, as good stewards of the manifold grace of God" (1 Pet. 4:10).

CONTENTS FOR CONTENTMENT

Gifts from people you love become life's treasures! Little in life touches the heart more than a gift carefully chosen for you by someone you love. It is not the price of the gift but the expression of love that matters. It is not the type of gift but the character of the giver that is meaningful.

I treasure every gift given to me by my precious husband, Chuck. Some of his gifts have been expensive while others have not. Some of his gifts have been things I have longed for while others have been surprises. All of his gifts have been treasures, expressions of his love for me. Some of his gifts have been beautifully wrapped by professionals while some have been wrapped simply with his own hands. All have been treasures because he chose them especially for me. As the giver, Chuck's responsibility is selecting the best gifts for me. As the receiver, I must graciously accept his gifts as tokens of his love.

My first Christmas present from Chuck was a brand-name electric mixer. While I was surprised and initially disappointed, I realized that he carefully selected that gift because of my frustration with an inadequate portable mixer. For my thirtieth birthday, Chuck compiled a book of letters from family and friends. I frequently reread those sweet notes. For my fortieth birthday, which I dreaded, Chuck celebrated for twelve days from my actual birth date until Christmas Day. I looked forward to each day. For our twenty-fifth wedding anniversary, he gave me something silver on the twenty-first day of every month for the entire year. My husband who loves me so much chooses gifts just for me. His gifts bring joy to me. Chuck carefully selects them, and I willingly accept them.

God, our heavenly Father, is a great gift-giver. He carefully selects spiritual gifts for each of His children. Each gift is personally chosen to bring glory to God and to give purpose to life.

What do you understand to be the definition of a spiritual gift? Write a definition in your own words right here.

_____

_____

_____

_____

_____

The Bible teaches many truths about spiritual gifts. In this lesson, you will examine numerous Scriptures which can help you be truly satisfied with the gifts God has given you. First, let's understand how the Bible defines a spiritual gift. The actual term *spiritual gift* is used often by the apostle Paul in the New Testament (Rom. 1:11; 1 Cor. 12:1, 14:1). The Greek word *pneumatidon* is actually translated *"spiritual gifts"* while the Greek word *charismaton* means *"grace gifts."* Both New Testament nouns have the same meaning but emphasize different truths. These are spiritual gifts given by a gracious God to His undeserving children.

In his book *Discover Your Spiritual Gift and Use It,* Rick Yohn gives a clear definition: *"Spiritual gifts are special abilities that God gives you to accomplish His work"* (Yohn, p. 3). Peter Wagner adds another insight in his book *Your Spiritual Gifts Can Help Your Church Grow:* *"A spiritual gift is a special attribute given by the Holy Spirit to every member of the Body of Christ according to God's grace for use within the context of the Body"* (Wagner, p. 42). Thayer's *Greek-English Lexicon of the New Testament* offers this definition of spiritual gifts: *"extraordinary powers, distinguishing certain Christians and enabling them to serve the church of Christ, the reception of which is due to the power of divine grace operating in their souls by the Holy Spirit."* (p. 667). For the purpose of this study, let's agree that a spiritual gift is a special ability that God gives to certain members of the body of Christ to be used for ministry and service.

Just understanding the definition of a spiritual gift can give a believer cause for contentment. God the Creator gives extraordinary abilities to His children for His kingdom's work. Believers are uniquely equipped to minister to others. However, the Bible teaches even more about spiritual gifts. Let's study a few other biblical truths. Spiritual gifts are gifts from God, gifts in variety, and gifts for service. For a believer those are important reasons to be content.

GIFTED BY GOD

Spiritual gifts are given to believers by God who loves them. One of the most consistent teachings of the Bible is the source of all spiritual gifts. **Read the following Scriptures to confirm who is the giver of spiritual gifts. The fact that God loves you so much that He has carefully chosen spiritual gifts for you can give you great satisfaction and joy.**

Acts 2:38—"Then Peter said to them, '...you shall receive the gift of the Holy Spirit.' "

Romans 12:3—"As God has dealt to each one a measure of faith."

1 Corinthians 12:7—"But the manifestation of the Spirit is given to each one for the profit of all."

Ephesians 4:11—"And He Himself gave some to be apostles, some prophets, some evangelists, and some pastors and teachers."

1 Peter 4:10—"...as good stewards of the manifold grace of God."

Each of these passages discusses spiritual gifts. Each one consistently identifies the giver of the gifts: God the Holy Spirit is the sole source of our spiritual gifts. In addition to the origin of gifts, the Bible also states clearly who receives the gifts. The following Scriptures identify the recipient.

After you read the verses below, fill in the blanks with the exact word or words used to pinpoint the receiver of God's spiritual gifts.

Romans 12:3 _____

1 Corinthians 12:7 _____

Ephesians 4:7 _____

1 Peter 4:10 _____

The Bible consistently identifies the believer as the only receiver of God's grace gifts. One must have a personal relationship with Jesus Christ in order to be gifted to serve Him. At the time of salvation, the believer receives the Holy Spirit and His appointed gifts. In addition, spiritual gifts are given to *every* believer. The Scripture assures this truth *"to everyone"* (Rom. 12:3) and *"to each one"* spiritual gifts are given (1 Cor. 12:7; Eph. 4:7, 1 Pet. 4:10). Whether you feel gifted or not, if you are a believer, God has given you a spiritual gift according to His will.

God not only selects the spiritual gift to impart to each believer, He selects them uniquely. He gives each believer at least one gift. To some, He gives many gifts. Spiritual gifts among believers are diverse. The expressions of those gifts vary widely, reflecting the creativity of God's children.

Several key passages in the New Testament identify spiritual gifts. While these lists are not intended to be comprehensive, they illustrate the types of gifts given by God to His children for the benefit of the kingdom.

As you read the Scriptures below, list each spiritual gift cited in the passage so you can see the diversity of gifts given by God.

Romans 12:6–8 _____

1 Corinthians 12:8–10 _____

1 Corinthians 12:28–30 _____

1 Corinthians 13:1–3 _____

Ephesians 4:11–16 _____

1 Peter 4:9–10 _____

GIFTED WITH VARIETY

Paul devoted much of his writing to the topic of spiritual gifts. He discussed in several epistles the different gifts and their functions. In Romans 12:6–8 he cited prophecy, ministry, teaching, exhortation, giving, leading, and mercy. These spiritual gifts are necessary for the body of Christ to function effectively. In 1 Corinthians 12:8–10, Paul repeated a few gifts but included others: wisdom, knowledge, faith, healing, miracles, prophecy, discernment, tongues, and interpretation. The same God gives all these gifts according to His will. In 1 Corinthians 12:28–30, Paul suggested positions within the church that are dependent upon specific spiritual gifts: apostles, prophets, teachers, miracles, healing, helps, administrations, and tongues. No spiritual gift or position in ministry is greater. All are equally important to God and His work.

The three remaining passages also address types of spiritual gifts. In 1 Corinthians 13, Paul mentioned numerous gifts by name: prophecy, knowledge, faith, giving, wisdom, and mercy. Here he emphasized the importance of love in utilizing all of these spiritual gifts. In Ephesians 4:11, Paul again recorded gifted individuals: apostles, prophets, evangelists, pastors, and teachers. In a final key passage, the apostle Peter included a spiritual gift enjoyed by many Christian women, the gift of hospitality. Each of these spiritual gifts is possessed by some believer, though no believer has them all.

Spiritual gifts are as diverse as God and as varied as His children. His gifts are used by His children for worshiping, for teaching, for serving, and for witnessing. No gift is greater than another. No one gift should be sought by all. All spiritual gifts are equal in the eyes of God just as each of His children is equal in worth and value. God chooses each gift, not to elevate the believer, but to accomplish His purpose.

Women easily admire the spiritual gifts of others. In fact, at times I don't feel gifted at all when I compare myself to others. I have even said, "I don't have any spiritual gifts." That is not true. God has given me spiritual gifts because I am a believer. I have often found the spiritual gifts of others more appealing to me than my own. *If only I could sing like Carol or speak like Linda or witness like Mary*, I think.

However, I am Rhonda, created in the image of God, uniquely gifted by the One who loves me. I can be content only when I accept those gifts given by God especially to me. After all, He gave me my gifts for a purpose. I want to receive them graciously and use them faithfully. When you come to that same conclusion, you can experience contentment.

GIFTED FOR SERVICE

Spiritual gifts are given by God in variety. While they are not to be sought selfishly, they are to be discovered and developed for ministry. God, who bestowed each gift specifically to every believer, gave them for a divine purpose, *"for the profit of all"* (1 Cor. 12:7). This purpose was supported by the apostle Peter: *"As each one has received a gift, minister it to one another, as good stewards of the manifold grace of God"* (1 Pet.

4:10). If you desire to use the gifts given to you by God wisely, you must minister them to others.

Ephesians 4:11–16 is an extended passage that discusses the purpose of spiritual gifts. After listing several spiritual gifts, Paul clearly describes how these gifts are to be used.

Carefully read Ephesians 4:11–16 and cite below the three-fold purpose of spiritual gifts. Gifts are to be used to:

_____

_____

_____

_____

Scripture teaches that spiritual gifts are given to each believer to equip other believers, to do the work of ministry, and to build up the body of Christ. Every spiritual gift is intended to strengthen the faith of believers, bring unity to the kingdom, and develop the body of Christ.

As spiritual gifts are employed, believers teach doctrine, serve others, and glorify God. Only as each believer faithfully uses her spiritual gifts is the body of Christ effective in doing its kingdom work. That is both a great privilege and a great responsibility. God chooses to use us to accomplish His purpose. What joy comes in knowing that God has purpose for our lives!

Spiritual gifts are clearly given by God in variety for service. These gifts are unique for each believer and differ from personal talents.

Can you think of some ways that spiritual gifts and natural talents vary? Compare them below.

<u>Spiritual Gifts</u>	vs.	<u>Natural Talents</u>

While spiritual gifts are given by God and are independent of parents, natural talents which are also given by God often come through parents. Spiritual gifts follow new birth or salvation while talents develop from birth. Spiritual gifts are intended for ministry to others while talents are for enjoyment by self and others. Spiritual gifts are discovered and developed in God's power while talents are discovered and developed in a person's own power. Spiritual gifts are a supernatural ability. Talents can be a tool used in service of those abilities. Therefore, spiritual gifts result in glory to God while natural talents may bring glory only to self.

Spiritual gifts differ from natural talents. Spiritual gifts also differ from the fruit of the Spirit. While all believers are to manifest the fruit of the Spirit or attributes of godly living (see Gal. 5:22–23), God chooses to give spiritual gifts in diversity to every believer. The Spirit is the source of His fruit and His gifts although the purposes are different. The fruit of the Spirit reflect spiritual growth in the life of the believer while spiritual gifts are the vehicles used by believers to minister to others. It has been said that spiritual gifts have to do with service while the fruit of the Spirit has to do with character.

If you have not completed a comprehensive study of spiritual gifts, you should do so. As you understand the gifts of God, you experience joy and purpose in life. You can also be used by God to encourage others to discover their spiritual gifts. Help others understand that God is the gift giver; He gives gifts at His own discretion; He gives gifts to every believer; He gives gifts for the purpose of ministry; and His gifts bring glory to Him. Like Paul, long to share spiritual gifts with others so that they may grow in their faith and be used in ministry (Rom. 1:11).

God, our loving Father, is the gracious giver of our spiritual gifts. We, His beloved children, must gratefully receive His gifts, develop them effectively, and use them faithfully. You can experience great satisfaction in knowing that God loves you so much that He wants to bestow on you supernatural abilities needed for His work on earth. You can receive great joy as you realize that your unique gifts are necessary for accomplishing God's purpose. You can be content as you accept your spiritual gifts given by God in variety for service.

CUSTOMIZE CONTENTMENT

Now that you have studied what the Bible teaches about spiritual gifts, you should be content with the Giver, with the gift, and with the good. Do you have a better understanding of your own spiritual gifts? Record below you specfic spiritual gifts and how you plan to use them.

What	**How**

"Be content with such things as you have" (Heb. 13:5).

Some things in life cannot be changed. One that cannot be changed is the family into which you were born. You have no control over your family of origin or the circumstances of your birth. Those decisions were made for you, and your response must be acceptance. When you accept your family as God's provision of love for you, you will be grateful.

The Bible teaches that marriage includes a permanent commitment. Once a Christian has married, that marriage should last a lifetime. While there may be things about your husband you would like to change, accepting him for who he is and focusing on his positive traits are best. Your marriage to a godly man can be a wonderful blessing to you.

If God brings children into your marriage, you need to accept them and their unique personalities. While those children you love may do things you do not love, you should forgive them and love them unconditionally. Your acceptance of your children can strengthen their character and satisfy your soul.

You may have a large extended family including brothers, sisters, aunts, uncles, nieces, and nephews. Each family member can be special to you if you accept them for who they are. Be careful not to put unrealistic expectations on members of your family. Work to spend time together. Keep in touch even when separated by distance.

As a Christian, accepting your family—your parents, your spouse, your siblings, and your relatives—is important. Family members are all God's children, created in His image and for His purpose. Accepting your role in the place where your family lives together is also essential. A home should be a haven of rest in this very hectic world. Your happiness with your home should not be dependent on its size or appearance. A Christian woman can make any house, apartment or dorm room a home by adding touches of love. Be content with the place where you live. Make that house a home of love for yourself, your family, and your friends.

CONTENTS FOR CONTENTMENT

A Christian woman must accept her family in order to achieve satisfaction in life. Criticism of family and complaints about a house are causes for discontentment. God ordained the family as the foundational institution of the human society. God truly honors the woman who honors her family. He blesses the woman who like the Proverbs 31 woman is satisfied with her husband, her children, and her home. The Scripture says:

> *She watches over the ways of her household,*
> *And does not eat the bread of idleness.*
> *Her children rise up and call her blessed;*
> *Her husband also, and he praises her:*
> *"Many daughters have done well,*
> *But you excel them all."*
> *Charm is deceitful and beauty is passing,*
> *But a woman who fears the Lord, she shall be praised*
>   *(Prov. 31:27–30).*

YOUR MARRIAGE

This is a good time to measure your contentment in your marriage. Are you satisfied with your marriage? Are you more in love with your husband today than when you married? Are you growing in your relationship as a couple? If not, take time to renew your commitment to your marriage in the same way you renew your relationship with the Lord. Be sure to tell your husband of your renewed commitment. If you are not satisfied with your marriage, spend time in prayer asking God to rekindle that flame of love and restore that intimate bond of marriage. He can do it, and He wants to do it. God wants you to be content in your marriage for your entire lifetime.

In order to develop contentment in marriage, you may need to study a basic biblical teaching about marriage. God uses the husband-wife relationship to teach you how He wants to relate to you personally.

Read Ephesians 5:22–33 to understand how Christians are to relate to Christ and wives are to relate to their husbands. Now write your understanding of each relationship below.

Christ–Church

_____

_____

Husband–Wife

_____

_____

God gave a clear model for relationships in the Bible. First, He taught that Christ is the head of the church. He provides loving leadership through Christians who respond with voluntary submission. That is God's plan for Christ and His Bride, the church. That same relationship pattern is prescribed for marriage. The husband is to lovingly lead while the wife voluntarily submits. God's plan for marriage, which was instituted in the Garden of Eden, (Gen. 2:15–25) gives men and women complementary roles and responsibilities for healthy marriages. A healthy marriage results when a man and a woman, each committed to the Lord, are committed for life to each other as partners, companions, lovers, and friends. A healthy marriage has two contented partners, each one satisfied with both themselves and their spouse.

Thank the Lord for your marriage! Thank your husband for loving you and leading you. You can be content as you willingly follow the loving leadership of your husband. Contentment in your marriage brings glory to God and joy to you. It passes along a heritage of contentment to your children and a witness of love to the world.

YOUR CHILDREN

Mothers and their children are naturally connected. They have a unique bond of love that cannot be broken. No matter your age, Mom is still Mom. No matter how old or how tall your child is, that child is still your baby. A mother's love is a great source of contentment for parents.

Before we examine a few biblical teachings about parenting, think about your own children. If you do not have children, think of some children who are special to you.

How have you expressed your love to your children? What have you said to communicate your acceptance of them? Have you affirmed them for who they are, not just what they do? Write each child's name below. Then write a compliment you can give that child affirming the child's character.

Child	Compliment
_____	_____
	_____
	_____
	_____
_____	_____
	_____
	_____
_____	_____
	_____
	_____

If your *quiver is full* (Psalm 127:5), you may have to add lines to include all your children and compliments for them. God intends for parents to protect and provide for their children while also teaching and training them. Parental instruction is most effective when taught by example as well as by words and actions.

The Bible affirms the worth of children. From the moment of conception, children are a gift from the Lord, a precious creation. Parents are to model for their children a strong relationship with the Lord and the biblical pattern for marriage. Parents are to teach children spiritual truths and moral values through love and discipline. Parents are to promote independence in their children so they will later be responsible for their own behavior and decisions. The Bible teaches that parents are to lovingly lead their children while children are to honor and obey their parents. Parents who lovingly lead and are respectfully obeyed can be content.

I am grateful for parents who lovingly led me into adulthood. They led me to the Lord, into His church, and into His ministry. Now it is my turn to share that heritage with the next generation. God did not give Chuck and me our own children, but I must say, *"Our quiver is full."* We are blessed with nieces, nephews, children of friends, and children of our campus. All believers have the responsibility and privilege of nurturing the next generation. Find children you can love and pour your life into them. You can find personal contentment in those children, knowing they are the future, God's hope in a hopeless world. Be content with who they are and who God wants them to be.

YOUR RELATIVES

My husband tells me, "I love your in-laws." In other words, he loves his parents who have become my in-laws. That is easy to say for most of us because we know and love our own parents best. However, a married woman's acceptance of her husband's parents as her own is a great blessing. When people marry, God enlarges the family which, although it is a good thing, can be challenging. A person literally marries the whole family. When two very different extended families are merged in marriage, acceptance is essential. Believers need to accept all our relatives completely and love them unconditionally.

Your family is truly a treasure. Those who are related to you by blood or adoption or marriage will be constants in your ever-changing life. Shared experiences with loved ones bring stability and safety. A close-knit family, not material possessions, can bring great contentment.

The biblical plan for families began in Genesis with Adam, Eve, their sons, and their families. The legacy of families is recorded throughout the Old Testament in the genealogies of Noah, Abraham, Moses, and David. The psalmist recorded this praise for families:

"Behold, children are a heritage from the Lord, The fruit of the womb is His reward. Like arrows in the hand of a warrior, So are the children of one's youth. Happy is the man who has his quiver full of them; they shall not be ashamed, but shall speak with their enemies in the gate" (Psalm 127:3–5).

In the New Testament, the family is affirmed by Jesus and instructed by Paul. The godly family not only strengthened its own members but ministered to others in God's name. God blesses those families who follow His biblical plan.

Read Colossians 3:18–25 then complete the sentences below with God's instructions through the apostle Paul to families.

Wives, submit to your own husbands, _____
_____ **(v. 18).**

Husbands, love your wives and _____
_____ **(v. 19).**

Children, obey your parents in all things, _____
_____ **(v. 20).**

Fathers, do not provoke your children, _____
_____ **(v. 21).**

And whatever you do, do it heartily, _____
_____ **(v. 23).**

Knowing that from the Lord you will receive the reward of the inheritance; _____ **(v. 24).**

God's plan for families is love, submission, obedience, and respect. When a family loves each other wholeheartedly, God is pleased, and He rewards the family abundantly. A godly family receives immediate blessings and eternal rewards. Though living together in love may be a challenge for families, it is well worth the effort. There is great contentment in being a part of a loving family. For a Christian, there is also great joy in being a part of the family of God.

In her book, *Gateways to Happiness,* Mary Lou Retton, the Olympic gymnast, identifies family as the first gateway to a more satisfying life. From birth, family can provide support and stability for an individual trying to become a healthy, happy adult. Family can continue to nurture and satisfy, but it takes work. Retton suggests three simple guidelines for keeping your family strong (pp. 34–40).

1. Be vocal about your affection. Regularly express your love in words.
2. Don't get caught up in petty disagreements. Resolve conflict immediately.
3. Appreciate your loved ones while you can. Reach out to them daily.

These suggestions can help all of us be content with our relatives.

YOUR HOME

I have always tried to make every place we have lived comfortable. Whether it was our 60-square-foot seminary apartment or the 6,000-square-foot President's House, our home has always been our haven of rest. I experience no greater joy than hearing from my husband what he feels in his heart when he drives in our carport after being away from home. He says a calm comes over his soul. Christian women should not only be contented themselves with their homes but should help their families be content too.

On a separate sheet of paper, draw a picture of your house. What does your home look like to you?

A house is one of the first pictures I learned to draw as a child. Even in its imperfect state, my house was always two stories high, with four windows and a door, plus a very tall roof with a chimney. My picture was never complete without a big tree and some colorful flowers, a few puffy clouds, a bird, and a sun with a happy face. A home was always a cheerful place for me. As a child, I was blessed with a godly home even though my house didn't actually match the one pictured in my dreams. As an adult, I am blessed with a loving home and even with a two-story house with a chimney, flowers, and trees. Isn't God good? Though He may not give us everything we want, He wants us to be content in our homes.

You may not have memories of a loving home, but it is not too late. You have the opportunity to create for your family a home that can foster contentment. The woman is generally the one who determines the climate of the home. A cheerful wife promotes a happy home. A positive mother encourages joy in the family. The old saying is very true: "If Mama ain't happy, nobody's happy." Are you fostering a climate of contentment in your home?

Pictures in many women's magazines today make us long for huge homes, fancy furnishings, or gorgeous gardens. The Bible warns us not to be envious of things others have. In fact, one of the Ten Command-ments forbids us from coveting our neighbor's house (Ex. 20:17). When someone tells me they would love to live in our big, beautiful home, I quickly inform them that there are four bathrooms to clean. In other words, the things we dream of are not always what they seem. Dreams are often not realistic. God desires for us to be content with what we have, the homes we live in.

Carefully examine the following Scriptures which teach believers to be satisfied with their own possessions and resources.

Deuteronomy 7:25 *You shall not covet silver or gold . . . lest you be snared by it.*

Proverbs 28:16 *He who hates covetousness will prolong his days.*

Luke 12:15 *And He said to them, "Take heed and beware of covetousness, for one's life does not consist in the abundance of things he possesses."*

Romans 7:7 *I would not have known sin except through the law. For I would not have know covetousness unless the law had said, "You shall not covet."*

Ephesians 5:3–5 *But fornication and all uncleanness or covetousness, let it not even be named among you...no fornicator, unclean person, nor covetous man, who is an idolater, has any inheritance in the kingdom of Christ and God.*

What do each of these verses have in common? Write a summary of these biblical truths here.

_____

_____

_____

_____

The Bible is clear: Christians are not to covet. We are to be content with what we have. Covetousness is a sin that can enslave us. A covetous Christian will not prosper and will not receive an inheritance from the Lord. Though our society is materialistic and desires acquisition of more, a Christian's life should not be dependent upon an abundance of possessions. We should be content with what we have, satisfied with our homes.

The Word of God teaches Christians to *"be content with such things as you have"* (Heb. 13:5). Be content with your marriage; be content with your children; be content with your relatives; be content with your home. A Christian woman who accepts her family completely is a woman who can find contentment. Be content with *who* you have, not *what* you have, then you will be a witness of God's love to others.

Complete the family tree below by filling in the names of your relatives. As you write each name, thank God for your family. Then make plans to continue strengthening your family bonds.

Spouse _____

Siblings _____

_____

_____

Children _____

_____

_____

_____

_____

Others _____

_____

_____

_____

_____

CUSTOMIZE CONTENTMENT

"And having food and clothing, with these we shall be content" (1 Tim. 6:8).

CONTENTS FOR CONTENTMENT

The world today places much emphasis on money and possessions. In fact, society judges an individual's success based on the balance of her bank account, size of her house, or model of her car. Money is the ultimate goal for many people since money is the world's primary determiner of success. Getting caught up in the world's desire for money and accumulation of things is easy for Christians as well as others. That desire for more makes contentment with what you have impossible.

Christians were no different in the time of Jesus. Because people sought material things more than spiritual growth, Jesus warned about the love of money. He often used parables to teach spiritual truths through daily life experiences. These parables or spiritual stories totaled much of the four gospels and often focused on material things.

Why do you think Jesus taught with parables?

_____

_____

_____

Jesus Himself explained why He taught with parables. In Matthew 13:10–15 and Luke 8:9–10, Jesus answered the disciples' questions about His parables. He said, *"'I speak to them in parables, because seeing they do not see, and hearing they do not hear, nor do they understand'"* (Matt. 13:13). Parables were used by Jesus who had all knowledge to instruct people who had limited knowledge. The parables of Jesus help Christians today understand God's teachings about money.

Read the following parables of Jesus about money. Then summarize a spiritual truth for each one.

Parable	Scripture	Spiritual Truth
Pearl of Great Price	Matt. 13:45–46	
The Talents	Matt. 25:14–30	
The Rich Fool	Luke 12:13–17	
The Lost Coin	Luke 15:8–10	
The Unjust Steward	Luke 16:1–13	

These parables teach us what our attitude toward money should be and how to accept our finances. Jesus clearly told His disciples that the gospel was of more value than any other thing (Matt. 13:45–46), and His children were to wisely use what God had given them (Matt. 25:14–30). In Luke, Jesus' parables instructed His followers to accumulate spiritual riches and not earthly treasures (Luke 12:13–17), to remember that Christ rejoices over a sinner who repents more than a lost coin that is found (Luke 15:8–10), and to be faithful with what they have, whether it is little or much (Luke 16:1–13). These same biblical principles apply to Christians today.

Christians must invest their time growing in the Lord rather than building up their bank accounts. We must trust the Lord to provide for our needs and be good stewards of what He has given us. We must share what we have with others and invest our lives in the spread of the gospel. If we can practice these spiritual truths, we will be content with our finances.

BE GRATEFUL FOR GOD'S PROVISION

Second to Jesus, Paul spoke more about money than any other contributor to the New Testament. As a part of his teachings about the Christian life, Paul encouraged believers to acknowledge God as the Giver of all things and to avoid greed for material possessions. Let's focus on one passage in the first letter to Timothy that clarifies how believers should consider money. First Timothy 6:6–10 teaches three truths: be grateful for God's provision, be content and not greedy, and be rich in good works. Consider these the three Be-attitudes about money.

Open your Bible and carefully read 1 Timothy 6:6–10. Now decide if the following statements about material possessions are true or false. Circle T for true and F for false, then correct the false statements.

T F   1. **Wealth with many possessions is great gain.**
            Correct: _____

T F   2. **Material possessions are only temporary.**
            Correct: _____

T F   3. **Be content when your basic needs are met.**
            Correct: _____

T F   4. **Desire for riches leads to prosperity.**
            Correct: _____

T F   5. **The love of money is the root of all kinds of evil.**
            Correct: _____

The Bible teaches that all you have has come from God and will be returned to Him. Therefore, you should respond with gratitude and good stewardship. Godliness with contentment brings great gain, not wealth and possessions (1 Tim. 6:6). Material possessions are only temporary. You were born with nothing and will die with nothing (1 Tim. 6:7). In other words, you cannot take the things you accumulate with you when you die. Rather than seeking your desires, you should be content when God provides your food and clothing, your basic needs (1 Tim. 6:8). Paul's warning is clear: avoid the greedy pursuit of riches. You will be tempted by the world to desire more (1 Tim. 6:9). An insatiable appetite for money will lead to your destruction. Do not love money more than you love God. A focus on money leads to sinfulness through many different kinds of evil (1 Tim. 6:10). You must focus on the Giver, God, rather than the gift, possessions.

In the Sermon on the Mount, Jesus taught His disciples to seek first the kingdom of God knowing He would provide what is needed for life (Matt. 6:33). What do you value? What do you seek first? When your focus is on the Provider, you don't have to worry about your provisions. When you are confident in God, you can be content with your finances.

Read the following verses as a reminder that God will provide for all of your needs because He loves you, not because you deserve anything.

Deuteronomy 10:14 *Indeed heaven and the highest heavens belong to the Lord Your God, also the earth with all that is in it.*

Psalm 24:1–2 *The earth is the Lord's, and all its fullness, the world and those who dwell therein. For He has founded it upon the seas, and established it upon the waters.*

Acts 17:25 *Nor is He worshiped with men's hands, as though He needed anything, since He gives to all life, breath, and all things.*

2 Corinthians 3:5 *Not that we are sufficient of ourselves to think of anything as being from ourselves, but our sufficiency is from God.*
Your response to God's generosity should not be a desire for more but a deep gratitude for what you have. God knows your needs and will always take care of you.

I love to shop! I must confess that shopping is one of my favorite pastimes. In fact, my husband likes to tease that shopping is one of my spiritual gifts! Buying is not what satisfies me. The process of looking relaxes me. I do pray often that God will keep my passion for possessions under control. Truthfully, my prayer is more often for God to control my husband who would love to buy everything for me. Rather than desiring more, I must be grateful for all that God has given me. He has blessed me abundantly, beyond what I could have ever asked or wished. God our Provider is like that. He loves to take care of His children.

The faithful provision of God has always been evident in my life. Chuck and I have had times in our marriage when we wondered how we would pay our bills. Our money has often run out before the month's end. As our finances got tighter, our faith got stronger. At the seminary, many personal testimonies are given telling how God provided when finances were scarce. A tax refund at the right time, a gift of money for a birthday, a check in the mail from a Christian friend are all ways God provides for our needs supernaturally. When you receive a gracious gift from God, be grateful for His provision and content with your checkbook.

BE CONTENT, NOT GREEDY

Though most Christians understand that everything comes from God, because of their human nature, they rarely are satisfied with what they have. It is typical for people to want more. This natural instinct is called *greed*. Greed is an insatiable desire for more money and more material things. In the Bible, greed is called *covetousness* which means *"the inordinate desire to possess what belongs to another"* (Butler, p. 313). In the Old Testament, the children of God are commanded not to covet another person's possessions (Ex. 20:17). In the New Testament, believers were told not to covet things which do not matter (Luke 12:15). Christian behavior is not characterized by greed. Instead, a Christian's response to material resources should be contentment (1 Thess. 2:5; 1 Tim. 3:3–8). God's children are to be content not greedy.

Look again at the passage in 1 Timothy 6:6–10. Paul firmly condemns greed and its snares. *"Those who desire to be rich fall into temptation and a snare...which drown men in destruction and perdition."* This passage records five warnings about the love of money. List those warnings below:

1. _____
2. _____
3. _____
4. _____
5. _____

The love of money, or greed, is the root or cause of all kinds of evil. Though greed may seem innocent at first, it leads to destruction. A greedy person can never get enough. She has an unquenchable thirst for more. Greed is like a cancer, spreading sinfulness to all parts of the body. Greed invades a person's life and consumes contentment. Be warned. The Scriptures teach: do not covet; do not be greedy. Do not even begin seeking things that are not of God. The first taste of selfishness is the beginning of greed.

Paul's warnings are clear in 1 Timothy 6:6–10. Greed is futile since we came into the world with nothing and will leave with nothing (v. 6). Greed leads to temptation, and insatiable desire makes a person susceptible to sin (v. 9). Greed brings destruction and eternal damnation, separation from God forever (v. 9). Greed is the root of all evil, and greed results in many sorrows (v. 10). While greed is a desire for greater satisfaction, it actually leads to deeper sorrow. A Christian who is greedy cannot be content.

In the 1960s and early 1970s my father was a well-known evangelist. God blessed his ministry, and he achieved great success. However, in the late 1970s, my father left the Lord for the lure of the world. He bought into the world's view of success, money and material possessions. The more possessions he acquired, the more he wanted. He left his first love of the Lord and began to love himself and his things. Now that he has returned to the Lord, my father will tell you that power, position, and possessions led to his fall. While he chose to love mammon (wealth and riches) rather than God, he never expected the consequences. His desire for riches caused him to fall into temptation, foolish and harmful lusts which drowned him in destruction. As Paul had warned, my father personally experienced that the love of money is a root of all kinds of evil. How grateful we are that my father has returned to the Lord, that he has been forgiven and restored. His testimony today warns others of the temptation and destruction of greed. Hear his message: be content with what you have, and do not be greedy.

BE RICH IN GOOD WORKS

Paul follows his warning about greediness with a positive admonition. He challenges the rich to use their money to do good for others, always being ready to give willingly. (See 1 Tim. 6:17–19.) When God blesses with riches, He expects generous giving. Jesus also taught that treasures are to be invested in eternal things: *"Do not lay up for yourself treasures on earth"* (Matt. 6:19–21). Those who love the Lord should serve others unselfishly, sacrificing all that they have to help those in need. Yes, the Bible does teach that God's children are to be rich—rich or extravagant in good works.

One of the Bible's most powerful accounts is the story of the woman who gave all she had, the widow with two mites. While she had little money, she was rich in good works. She willingly gave what she had for the benefit of others.

Read the story of the widow with two mites recorded in Mark 12:41–44. What did Jesus say to affirm the woman's sacrificial gift?

_____

_____

Though the total of her gift was little, the sacrifice of her heart was great. She sincerely gave all she had while the Pharisees arrogantly gave only part of their possessions. Notice the significant contrast between the humble widow and the wealthy worshipers. The widow reminds believers today that everything we have belongs to God. We should generously give our all. While giving from the surplus is easy, giving our all is godly. Give to others, and be rich in good works.

As a child, my Christian parents taught me to tithe, to give the first tenth of my earnings to the church for the Lord's work. Even when my allowance was small, the lesson was profound. My parents also challenged me to sacrificially give offerings to others. I confess that I was not always eager to share my money, but I learned that God blessed me abundantly when I gave cheerfully. When Chuck and I married, we began our family budget with tithes and offerings. Though our income was limited, God stretched our wallets as we willingly gave. Even now, we are blessed when we respond to the needs of others with a check or with cash. That is what being rich in good works means—not just generous in giving money, but gracious in sharing resources, talents, and time. Christians are to be serious stewards of all they have (1 Pet. 4:10). God who holds us accountable wants us to accept our finances.

Jesus wants us to be content with our finances. He wants us to see and hear and understand what He is teaching: God provides generously; God discourages greediness; and God desires your giving to others from what you have. What valuable truths! What spiritual insights! Believers can be content with their finances because God is in control. Contentment in life includes satisfaction with your financial status. Let God who is in control give you contentment as you live.

CUSTOMIZE CONTENTMENT

Take a moment for personal inventory. Are you really content having your needs met? Or are you most comfortable with those things you want? List below some material possessions that you could give up.

_____

_____

_____

How would letting go of these simplify your life?

_____

_____

_____

"For I have learned in whatever state I am, to be content" (Phil. 4:11).

CONTENTS FOR CONTENTMENT

Christians would love to think that from the time of salvation they would have no more problems, that the life of a believer is filled only with joy and no sorrow. However, reality is a harsh reminder that life, even for the believer, includes daily challenges, painful conflicts, and difficult circumstances. The Bible is honest about this fact. The Bible encourages believers to be content in all circumstances and to allow God to use those circumstances for good (Rom. 8:28). For the believer, God sustains and strengthens through even the most painful circumstances. Because of God's unfailing love and faithful presence, Christians can be content in their circumstances.

My husband, Chuck, says it this way: "The circumstances of your life are not a comment on what God thinks about you. The cross is God's statement of how much He loves you and how determined He is to care for you." While life's circumstances can seem overwhelming, God's love overpowers them all. Christians may ask tough questions like "Why did this happen to me?" or "Where was God when this happened?" The answer is simple. God was there. He is ever-present and all-knowing. He is also all-loving. God loves His children so much that He sent His Son to provide salvation through His death on the cross. That act of love is an assurance to believers of God's devoted care and deep concern. While the circumstances of life can still cause pain for the believer, the cross soothes the pain and heals the broken heart. Do you believe that? Have you experienced God's love during your tough circumstances?

As we consider personal circumstances, reflect on your own life. Has there been a time in your life when your circumstances caused great suffering to you personally? If not yet, you will someday face those challenges. The Bible speaks the truth that trials come. It is not a matter of if but of when (James 1:2). Pray that God will prepare you for those difficulties. If you have experienced painful circumstances, remember God's love for you during that time of hurt. Write here what you learned through those circumstances.

I was a young adult before I experienced a truly devastating circumstance in my life. In fact, my life seemed perfect when the tragedy hit. Raised in a Christian family, I married a godly man, and we were preparing for ministry when my parents divorced. What made the divorce even more painful was the fact that my dad was an evangelist and my spiritual hero. At a time when my life circumstances could have destroyed me, I learned to be content in the midst of my circumstances. That is when God taught me personally about His presence, His sovereignty, and His redemption. My colleagues did not understand how I could continue to work under the pressure. Even my Christian friends did not understand how I could have such peace in such pain. I understood clearly for the first time that my faith was not in my father but in God. When you focus on God even when your circumstances are challenging, you can be content because of your relationship with Him.

Recently I have been encouraged by the strong faith of family and friends who have faced trials. One friend who is alone now after divorce said that she can literally feel the loving arms of the Lord around her. She depends on Him for strength and companionship. Another friend whose husband left her told me how she experiences the presence and power of God in her pain. She said that she can actually hear the murmurings of Christian friends praying for her. God and His children are a support during times of suffering. Chuck's parents experienced strength from the Lord during a most difficult year while his father battled cancer, they moved from their hometown of 53 years, and his mother left her dearest friends. Even when life is turned upside down, Christians can be content in their circumstances.

GOD RECOGNIZES YOUR CIRCUMSTANCES

In one of his New Testament letters, Paul encouraged Christians to meditate on some biblical truths. Paul learned to apply these truths in his own life full of serious challenges. He knew that Christians had heard and seen those things, but they needed to practice them personally as he had. Paul learned to be content in every circumstance of life as God strengthened him. Because of God, he could live above things, his spirit could be unaffected by his circumstances. Let's study the Scripture to see how God recognizes, rules over, and redeems all circumstances in our lives. Then we as Christians can be content.

While the word *circumstances* includes all events or happenings of life, most people struggle only with those events or circumstances that are difficult or challenging. Rejoicing is easy when things are going well. Celebrating joyous occasions and personal accomplishments is natural. However, a Christian must learn to be content in all circumstances, good or bad, happy or sad. In fact, the faith of a Christian may be strengthened more during tough times than in easy times.

Turn to Philippians 4. Paul the Apostle wrote this letter from a prison in Rome to the Christians in Philippi about their faltering faith. He reminded them of God's presence and power in his own life. He encouraged them to depend on God even in distress.

Read Philippians 4:10–13, 19. Take a few minutes to identify the statements used by Paul to reinforce the care and provision of God for His children. List them below.

_____
_____
_____
_____
_____

These words of Paul are comforting during times of crisis: *"you surely did care"* (v. 10), *"I have learned ... to be content"* (v. 11), *"I know how to abound"* (v. 12), *"I have learned both to be full"* (v. 12), *"Christ who strengthens me"* (v. 13), and *"God shall supply all your need"* (v. 19). These biblical truths foster contentment in Christians because they confirm that God is always present in every circumstance.

In the late nineteenth century, Hannah Whitall Smith answered the question "Is God in everything?" in her book, *The Christian's Secret of a Happy Life*. She concluded that the Christian's confidence that God is in everything is what brings joy. Whether good or bad, all circumstances of life pass through the hands of our loving God who is aware of what is happening and concerned about the outcome. No circumstance occurs without the knowledge and permission of God. He is actively involved in the events of our lives. Smith summarized her conviction with this statement, *"Seeing our Father in everything makes life one long thanksgiving, and gives a rest of heart, and, more than that, a gayety* [sic] *of spirit that is unspeakable"* (Smith, p. 157). You can echo this chorus of contentment.

Numerous other Scriptures affirm God's presence and work in the world. God has always been present, and He will always be present. He created everything and is in everything. God is omnipresent. He is present among His people and in relationships. God is present with us to help us and to strengthen us. The psalmist frequently thanked God for His presence.

"You will show me the path of life; in Your presence is fullness of joy; at Your right hand are pleasures forevermore" (Psalm 16:11).

"For You have made him most blessed forever; You have made him exceedingly glad with Your presence" (Psalm 21:6).

"God is our refuge and strength, a very present help in trouble" (Psalm 46:1).

"Serve the Lord with gladness; come before His presence with singing" (Psalm 100:2).

"Where can I go from Your Spirit? Or where can I flee from Your presence?" (Psalm 139:7).

GOD RULES OVER YOUR CIRCUMSTANCES

The New Testament also proclaims the presence of God. God came to earth as man in the person of Jesus Christ so He could be present with us (John 1:14). After the death of Jesus, God remained with us in the person of the Holy Spirit (John 14:16–17). God continues to be with us at all times in all situations. That knowledge is why we can rejoice. The writer of Hebrews reminded us that *"He Himself has said, 'I will never leave you nor forsake you'"* (Heb.13:5). Therefore, we can be content. His constant presence assures us that God recognizes our circumstances, He is aware of our experiences, and He rules over our circumstances.

All circumstances of life are under the control of God, the Sovereign Ruler. God the Creator not only rules over His creation, but God the Father rules over His children and their life experiences. At the time of conversion, a believer submits herself to the complete authority of God over her life. She is dependent on Him and accountable to Him and will be for eternity. God's sovereign rule over people is expressed in loving concern. He is aware of their problems, and He knows the solutions. How reassuring to know that my life is not in my hands but in the hands of my Sovereign Lord who loves me and will care for me.

Carefully study one biblical passage about the sovereignty of God. Read 1 Chronicles 29:10–15. Fill in the blanks below from verse 12 to describe the rule of God.

"Both riches and honor come from _____.
And You _____ over all.
In Your hand is _____ and _____ ;
In Your hand it is _____ to make _____
And to give _____ to all."

David proclaimed the sovereignty of God to his people. He praised God for His greatness, power, glory, victory, and majesty (v. 11). He acknowledged that God is ruler of everything in both heaven and earth (v. 11). David realized that everything came from God and that He reigns over all (v. 12). According to David, God alone has the power and might to give strength to all (v. 12). This biblical evidence of God's sovereign rule over all people and things is a basis for the Christian's contentment in all circumstances. The sovereignty of God is worthy of praise and cause for contentment.

In a recent women's magazine, a journalist asked the question "What's keeping you from feeling happy?" She began her article with her own answer. She confessed that she was unhappy despite her apparent success.

This professional woman said she "had the trappings of what I thought success was—a high-paying corporate job; a nice car; a full social calendar"—but was still unfulfilled. Her conclusion amplifies the world's perspective. Happiness is dependent on personal effort alone. The body of her article suggested many changes she could make in her life, but still she was responsible for her own life. While Christians do make choices in life, God is responsible for His children. What an assurance to know that God rules over my life and my circumstances and further helps me be content.

God not only recognizes and rules over my circumstances but also redeems them. When something hurtful happens, our loving Father has the power to redeem it. The word *redemption* is one theological term every believer should understand. God's work of redemption begins in a Christian's life at the time of conversion and continues throughout life. The redeeming power of God is another cause for the Christian to be content in any circumstance.

The word *redeem* means *to exchange one thing for another.* In life, many things are exchanged. Coupons are exchanged for cash; bottle caps are exchanged for prizes; and customer cards are exchanged for free coffee. These items are redeemed. In the Christian life, sin is redeemed. Separation from God (sin) is exchanged for fellowship with God. Redemption is an ongoing work of God in the lives of sinful people. God chooses to redeem people and to redeem their circumstances. He can take bad experiences and exchange them for good. That, too, is called redemption. The redemptive work of God in His children is recorded often in Scripture. In His ministry on earth, Jesus brought redemption to many people including a number of women. He exchanged something bad in their lives for something good. For the hemorrhaging woman, Jesus exchanged sickness for health (Matt. 9:20–22). For the widow with two mites, He exchanged little for much (Mark 12:41–44). For Mary Magdalene, He exchanged bondage for freedom (Mark 16:9). For Jairus' daughter, He exchanged death for life (Luke 8:40–56). For the woman at the well, Jesus exchanged sinfulness for salvation (John 4:1–26). Jesus had the power to redeem every circumstance, every life challenge.

One of the most powerful examples of God's redemption is recorded in the Old Testament. The story of Joseph, a patriarch of Israel, is chronicled in the book of Genesis (Gen. 30:22–50:26). The favored son of Jacob, Joseph was sold into slavery by his jealous brothers. Later, he was imprisoned in Egypt on the false charge of rape. In both circumstances, God exchanged the bad in Joseph's life for something good. As Pharaoh's second in command, Joseph led Egypt successfully through a time of famine and confronted his brothers with their injustice. Instead of responding with revenge, Joseph offered forgiveness. He understood that God had redeemed the unfair circumstances in his life. The victim became the victor!

GOD REDEEMS YOUR CIRCUMSTANCES

Read Joseph's verdict issued to his brothers in Genesis 50:20: *"But as for you, you meant evil against me; but God meant it for good, in order to bring it about as it is this day, to save many people alive."* **What does that verse say to you about God's work in Joseph's life? Summarize this biblical truth right here.**

_____

_____

_____

_____

While Joseph's brothers intended to harm him, God protected him. He exchanged their violence for Joseph's safety. He exchanged something evil for something good. Joseph's circumstances were recognized by God, were ruled over by God, and were redeemed by God. As a result, Joseph was content in God's care.

The New Orleans seminary has an extension center in the state's maximum security prison for men. Prisoners serving life sentences are receiving a theological education. As many prisoners give their lives to the Lord, they want to grow in Him and serve Him. Some of them lead congregations of believers behind the bars. While many of the prisoners will never leave prison alive, they want to minister to their cellmates in the name of the Lord. Like Paul who was also imprisoned, these Christian inmates can share a message of spiritual freedom while they themselves are not physically free. What a testimony of God's redemptive grace! God exchanged what was evil in their lives for something good.

In a recent seminary graduation at the prison, the warden praised their accomplishments. He recognized that each graduate who had been a murderer was now a minister of the gospel. The completion of their degrees was for many a first-time success. With tears in their eyes, they received diplomas, symbols of God's redemptive work in their lives. Tears filled the eyes of all people present as God exchanged evil for something good.

GOD'S REDEMPTIVE POWER

God's redemptive power is evident in the lives of His children. In his book *The Road Most Traveled: Releasing the Power of Contentment in Your Life,* Robert Jeffress encourages readers to let God exchange disappointments in life for contentment. His premise is simple but profound: *"lasting satisfaction in life does not come from extraordinary events, but by learning to appreciate the unchangeable circumstances, choices, and even mistakes that shape our destiny"* (Jeffress, p. 8). For the Christian that means letting God redeem your life and your circumstances.

In Philippians 4:11, Paul recommended a response by Christians to all of life's circumstances. He said, "Be content!" He learned to be contented in every state. As a preacher once joked, "Paul could be content in Alabama, Arkansas, or Alaska." In simple words, be happy wherever you are and with whatever is happening. Paul did not let his circumstances control his attitude. Because his confidence was in Christ, he knew his circumstances were under control. Paul taught believers by example that contentment in all circumstances is possible because of the character of God. God recognizes your circumstances, He rules over your circumstances, and He redeems your circumstances. So be content!

In her book *Ashes to Gold,* Patti Roberts reflects on the exchange that took place in Job's life. Through the suffering in his life, Job experienced the redemption of God. The ashes of his life were exchanged for gold (Job 30:19). What evil in your life has God exchanged for good? Explain how.

_____

_____

_____

Thank Him for His redemptive work!

LESSON EIGHT   ACCEPTING YOUR LIFE'S WORK

"Do not intimidate anyone or accuse falsely, and be content with your wages" (Luke 3:14).

More women are in the workforce today than ever before. Professional women are employed in all careers and in most work settings. A portrait of the workplace includes the faces of many women. While many Christian women work outside the home, many also work inside the home. Whether paid or unpaid, employed or unemployed, all women work. The worth of a woman is not determined by her occupation or by her effort. Instead, the worth of a woman is determined by her relationship with God. He has created all people in His image, of equal value, and with different but worthwhile roles.

In the Bible, God teaches about work by His Word and His example. He affirms human labor though He cautions about worshiping work. In the *Holman Bible Dictionary,* T. R. McNeal suggests four major points in the theology of work:

1. God's people work because they are made in His image.
2. God's people reflect Him through practicing integrity in their work.
3. God's people realize His plan for work also includes a plan for rest.
4. God's people see their primary vocation as serving Him (pp. 1418–1419).

These guidelines help a Christian woman evaluate her work. Since we are made in the image of God, Christians should imitate His work habits. The Bible begins with an account of the work of God in creation. He continues to be at work in the world and in the lives of His children today. He created humans with the capacity to work, and He assigned specific jobs. God works diligently; so we should be hard-working. Christian employees need to be conscientious, honest, and cooperative in their work. This theology of work also includes some warnings: remember to rest and serve the Lord. God's pattern was for work and rest: *"He rested on the seventh day from all His work"* (Gen. 2:2). Workers need a time to reflect on God and to restore their energies. Christian workers must realize that one's most important work is serving the Lord. This biblical instruction about work is clear and convicting.

Now it is time to examine your own work. Why do you work? How do you work? Do you rest? Does your work include service? Take a few minutes to reflect on your work style. Then record below how you feel about your work. What kind of worker are you? ____

_____

_____

_____

While there are many Scriptures that teach about work, one Old Testament book focuses on work. Find Ecclesiastes in your Bible. Let's find what "the Preacher" or author of Ecclesiastes has to say about work. While many specific instructions are given for work, the attitude of the worker is primary. God desires for His children to have an attitude of contentment about their work. Christians should be content with their work, with their wages, and with their wealth.

CONTENT WITH YOUR WORK

The book of Ecclesiastes was probably written by King Solomon in the tenth century B.C. As wisdom literature, the book was written to educate the people. Its theme is the search for life's meaning. The author concluded that the meaning of life does not lie in labor, luxury, lust, leisure, learning, or liquor. He realized that life's meaning is found only in a relationship with the Lord (Eccl. 12:13–14). In his search, the author who identified himself as the Preacher, examined the significance of his work.

Read his feelings in Ecclesiastes 2:17–26. His words clearly reflect his feelings about his work. List a few of those descriptive words in the margin.

The Preacher chose some strong words to express his negative feelings about his work: hate, distress, toil, foolish, despair, grasping. His words are clear. The effort of our work may seem useless if we work for ourselves and not for the Lord. No wonder the Preacher was discontented. His work was for his own benefit, and he knew his efforts would be lost after his death. However, if our efforts are for God, then our energies are invested in eternal matters. That is a reason for Christians to be content.

All of us work hard at the seminary. We recently completed a major renovation project which required extra effort on the part of everyone. When workers became overwhelmed or discouraged, we reminded them to focus on the real reason for the work, God's command and His children who will help fulfill that Great Commission. The night before that building opened for classes, my precious husband knelt in the foyer on the seal that says "Go—make disciples—baptize—teach" and prayed this prayer of dedication: "Lord, this building is nothing but bricks and mortar. Bricks and mortar will never change a life, but the people who will study here can change the world." Our efforts in ministry have eternal significance. That is cause for contentment!

As a child, what did you want to be when you grew up? Some children changed their answers daily, but not me. I always wanted to be a teacher, probably because teachers get to talk! I pursued that goal in my education and then in my career, first as a speech pathologist and now as a teacher. One of the reasons I am content in my work is that I am doing what I always dreamed of doing. However, I am content in my work primarily because I am serving God and teaching His Word. I am confident that I am doing God's will for my life.

Many Christian women are not content with their work. It may be because they are not doing what they want to do or are not fulfilling their dreams. Like the Preacher, we can be content when we are doing our God-given tasks.

Read Ecclesiastes 3:9–13. You will notice the change in the writer's heart. While his work may not have changed, his attitude about his work has definitely changed. Can you echo the words of the Preacher?

"I know that there is nothing better for them than to rejoice, and to do good in their lives, and also that every man should eat and drink and enjoy the good of all his labor—it is the gift of God" (Eccl. 3:12–13).

Are you content in your work?

Christian women are to be content with their work both in the home and in the workplace. It is also important to be content with your wages. John the Baptist spoke these words to his new converts, *"Do not intimidate anyone or accuse falsely, and be content with your wages"* (Luke 3:14). His instructions to those young in the faith are also appropriate teachings for us today. We should be satisfied with the payment we receive, knowing that God will provide for our needs. Whether we have little or much, we should be grateful.

Rarely does a person feel they are paid what they are due. It is actually impossible to be compensated completely for the work that you do. Many people spend their time complaining about low pay instead of being content with their paycheck. God wants us to be satisfied with our work and our wages. We can be confident in His promise to provide.

I can only say that I am content with my wages and always have been. God has always taken care of me financially. Even when my salary was minimum wage, I was content. Even now, when I am not compensated financially for most of my work at the seminary, I am content. I know God will provide. Contentment with your wages results when you are confident in your calling. In other words, when you are fulfilling your God-given task, you can be content no matter what you are paid.

CONTENT WITH YOUR WAGES

At the seminary, we are blessed to have many faculty and staff who are content with their wages. In a secular job, their salaries could be six figures. In ministry, their compensation is much less. Because of confidence in their calling to theological education, they are content with their wages. God always provides for their needs. They share many testimonies of God's miraculous provision.

Return to the narrative of the Preacher in Ecclesiastes 4:4–8. Carefully read these two proverbs and answer the question, "What is the result of selfish toil?" In verses four, seven, and eight, the one-word answer is given: *vanity*. The Preacher often answers the questions about life with *"Vanity of vanities, all is vanity."* **What does vanity mean in response to the question about work?**

The Preacher uses the word *vanity* in the book of Ecclesiastes figuratively. Vanity describes something worthless, meaningless, and without substance. In other words, life and work are useless if they are lived for one's own gain. However, if life and labor are for the Lord and in accordance with His will, contentment is possible. The Preacher notes that skillful work for the sake of self-fulfillment is futile. Being satisfied with only a handful of money is better than to have an abundance of possessions and be motivated by envy. One thing is obvious, the Preacher found no satisfaction in the accumulation of money. He found contentment with his wages when he was committed to doing God's will.

CONTENT WITH YOUR WEALTH

Christian women can experience true happiness when they are content with their work, content with their wages, and content with their wealth. Wealth is a blessing from God, and wealth is a responsibility assigned by God. Wealth does not imply abundance or affluence in response to personal worth or achievement. Instead wealth is the material resource given by God to His children for His use. Human weakness may misuse wealth for personal gain and status. When viewed by Christians as a vehicle of God's work, wealth can be godly and good. The world around us perceives wealth to mean position and power.

In his devotional commentary on the book of Ecclesiastes, Warren Wiersbe notes four myths about wealth (*Be Satisfied,* pp. 67–71). He identifies them in Ecclesiastes 5:10–20.

Before you read the myths below, read Ecclesiastes 5:10–20. Understanding why wealth is not what the world proposes it to be is important. Earlier in his record, King Solomon discussed *the futility of wealth* (Eccl. 2:1–11). Then he dispelled several myths the people had about wealth. These are the myths about wealth that rob believers of the blessings from God.

Myth 1: "Wealth brings satisfaction" (v. 10). Many who are wealthy are miserable. They have found that money does not guarantee happiness. Only God can satisfy the human heart.

Myth 2: "Money solves every problem" (v. 11). While some money may be necessary for survival, money is not the solution to the world's problems. Often an increase in money only complicates life. God is the only answer to every problem.

Myth 3: "Wealth brings peace of mind" (v. 12). Solomon himself said that possessing wealth is no guarantee of sound sleep. A believer may sleep like a baby knowing she is safe in the arms of the Savior. Money does sedate. The provision of God is what satisfies the soul and promotes rest.

Myth 4: "Wealth provides security" (vv. 13–17). Wealth is fleeting. Money in your pocket today may be gone tomorrow. The stock market is a perfect example of the volatility of investments. One day the stocks are high, and the next day the stocks are low. The most secure investments are those stocks which perform well over time. For the Christian, life's greatest security is the Lord who always keeps His promises. The Preacher concludes that security results from enjoying all that God has given (Eccl. 5:18).

Remember Jesus' parables about money? He told of a wealthy man who depended solely on his money for security. **Read his story in Luke 12:13–21.**

Jesus taught people about covetousness by telling of a rich man who hoarded crops and goods that he could not take with him when he died. Jesus informed the people that a rich man who lays up treasure for himself is not rich at all. A man was truly wealthy when he was rich toward God. This parable of Jesus dispelled the myths about wealth.

In this lesson you have focused on work, wages, and wealth. **Can you create a parable that warns about dependence on personal wealth? Write your parable on a separate piece of paper.**

Contentment is one of life's greatest lessons to learn. Can you learn to be satisfied with the life God has given you? Can you be happy where you are, doing what you are doing? Can you be content when God meets your need but does not give your desires? Can you be satisfied with your wages though they do not adequately compensate your worth? Contentment is an important personal lesson to be learned and an essential life lesson to be taught to your children.

If you desire contentment, you must focus your eyes on the Lord in all matters of life, including your work. The Preacher discovered this truth as he closed his book: *"Fear God and keep His commandments, For this is man's all. For God will bring every work into judgment, including every secret thing, whether good or evil"* (Eccl. 12:13–14). The psalmist reminded people not to worship the works of their own hands (Psalm 115:1–8). The prophet Jeremiah warned God's children not to exalt the things created with their hands or to elevate them to the place of honor in their lives (Jer. 25:6–7). In the New Testament, this message was repeated by Paul: *"Speak, not as pleasing men, but God"* (1 Thess. 2:4). When we focus our eyes on the Worthy One rather than our work, wages, or wealth, we can truly be content.

Warren Wiersbe ended his discussion of Ecclesiastes 5 with a challenge to focus on God. **Read these words aloud as a commitment to God and a confidence in His good work.**

If we focus more on the gifts than on the Giver, we are guilty of idolatry. If we accept His gifts, but complain about them, we are guilty of ingratitude. If we hoard His gifts and will not share them with others, we are guilty of indulgence. But if we yield to His will and use what He gives us for His glory, then we can enjoy life and be satisfied (Wiersbe, p. 71).

In the fourth century A.D. the prominent theologian St. Augustine taught that delight in the Lord was the source of abundant Christian living. He challenged Christians to focus their hearts on God rather than their material possessions. In one dialogue, Augustine shared an example that powerfully illustrated his point that the Giver, not the gift, deserves our devotion. This illustration which refers to marital love is especially relevant to women. It is a profound challenge to love the Lord more than money.

Read Augustine's example below.

Suppose, brethren, a man should make a ring for his betrothed, and she should love the ring more wholeheartedly than the betrothed who made it for her . . . —Certainly, let her love his gift: but, if she should say, 'The ring is enough. I do not want to see his face again, what would we say of her? . . . The pledge is given her by the betrothed just that, in his pledge, he himself may be loved. God, then, has given you all these things. Love Him who made them (Piper, p. 71).

Hear the challenge of Augustine. Love God more than your work. Be content with the wages and wealth He has given you.

CUSTOMIZE CONTENTMENT

Now that you have carefully considered your own work and made a commitment to be content with your wages, take time to set some goals to enhance your work.

Identify three or four specific things you can do to be a good steward of your God-given work. List your goals below:

_____

_____

AVOIDING DISCONTENTMENT

"Oh, that we had been content, and dwelt on the other side of the Jordan!" (Josh. 7:7).

CONTENTS FOR CONTENTMENT

Discontentment is an emotional state that is hard to avoid. Being discontented and dissatisfied with life often seems easy. Negative thoughts and critical feelings are part of human nature. Also, the world bombards us with critiques, reviews, and evaluations, all harsh judgments. Even Christians can be negative, critical, or judgmental. Harsh words pop out of our mouths. Cruel actions become natural reflexes. Jealous thoughts fill our minds. God says we are to avoid discontentment. Paul said it this way in Ephesians 4:29: *"Let no corrupt word proceed out of your mouth, but what is good for necessary edification, that it may impart grace to the hearers."*

Before we examine the subject of discontentment, let's study the word itself. The prefix *dis-* often changes a root word to its opposite or negates the positive definition of the word. Thus *discontent* has the opposite meaning of *content.* Discontentment is not compatible with contentment. Discontentment is the state of unhappiness or dissatisfaction. Christians must avoid discontentment. With the help of the Lord, discontentment can be replaced by true contentment, genuine joy, and deep satisfaction.

Many *dis-* words reflect discontentment. Here is a selected list of negative feelings Christians should avoid.

disabled—incapable
disaffected—alienated
disagree—differ
disagreement—argument
disarrange—disturb
disavow—deny
disbelieve—reject
disclaim—renounce

disadvantaged—inferior
disaffirmed—contradicted
disagreeable—ill-tempered
disappoint—frustrate
disarray—confusion
disband—destroy
discharge—fire
disclose—reveal, expose

discolor—alter   discomfort—grieve
disconcert—embarrass   disconnect—terminate
discord—strife   discount—reduce
discourage—deprive   discredit—doubt
discriminate—prejudice   disdain—contempt
disendow—rob   disengage—withdraw
disestablish—remove status   disfavor—withhold
disfigure—impair   disgrace—shame
disgruntle—grumble, fuss   disharmony—lack of unity
dishearten—lose spirit   dishonest—deceitful
dishonor—humiliate   disillusion—lose heart
disincline—unwilling   disinherit—remove rights
disinterest—no concern   disinvest—reduce capital
disjoin—detach   dislike—aversion to
dislocate—force a change   disloyal—unfaithful
dismiss—remove   disobey—reject
disorder—disturb   disorient—confuse
disparage—degrade   dispel—drive away
disperse—scatter   displace—rearrange
displease—make unhappy   dispose—get rid of
dispraise—criticize   disprove—refute
dispute—oppose   disqualify—deem unfit
disquiet—alarm   disregard—neglect
disreputable—of low esteem   disrupt—interrupt
dissent—difference of opinion disservice—harm
dissipate—scatter   dissociate—reject
distance—move away from   distaste—feel aversion to
distortion—falsification   distract—divert attention
disturb—bother   disunite—separate
disuse—rid of   disvalue—depreciate

These *dis*-attitudes can be *dis*-astrous! So *dis*-card them from your life. *Dis*-continue them before they cause you undue *dis*-may and *dis*-tress. They will *dis*-solve your contentment and make you *dis*-satisfied!

Examine your own life. Have you allowed negative feelings to creep into you mind? Have you become critical or judgmental? These attitudes are ungodly and will not result in contentment. Confess this sin to the Lord. Determine to avoid discontentment. Write your prayer of commitment in the margin or on a separate sheet of paper.

SOURCES OF DISCONTENTMENT

You may have asked yourself: Where does my discontentment come from? What is the source of discontentment?

While people are different and circumstances vary, some common causes of discontentment can be discovered. Before we identify those, let's learn from a Bible character how to avoid discontentment. **Turn in your Bibles to Joshua 7:1–9. Read this lesson learned by a leader of the Israelites.** Joshua recognized his source of discontentment and repented of his ways.

Joshua attempted to lead his people, but they had disobeyed God and experienced His wrath. They were soundly defeated by the enemy and were very discouraged. Their discontentment led to Joshua's depression. In the depths of despair, he finally acknowledged: *"Oh, that we had been content, and dwelt on the other side of the Jordan!"* Joshua then cried out to God for help (Josh. 7:8). God told Joshua and the Israelites to get up, to repent, and to obey (Josh. 7:10–16). Then they experienced blessing again.

The Israelites' source of discontentment was their **sin**. Sin is a primary cause of discontentment in Christians. Simply defined, sin is separation from God. For a Christian to have joy in the Lord when separated from Him by sin is impossible.

Another helpful definition of sin is that sin is lack of fellowship with God. Anything that disturbs your relationship with God is sin. Sin, which results in guilt, causes discontentment. The psalmist David knew that contentment was dependent on a clean heart before God (Psalm 51). He confessed his sin, was restored in fellowship with God, and experienced satisfaction.

Another source of discontentment is **surroundings**. Living in a world of plenty and in a society of sinfulness can often make a believer discontent. A search for more, a pursuit of success, a desire for self-fulfillment, a temptation to sin are encouraged by surroundings. Though Christians are to be in the world but not of the world (1 John 2:15), the world can influence even the strongest Christian.

I learned personally the powerful influence of my surroundings in my first job. In the hospital setting where I worked, my colleagues were negative and critical. They were discouraged in their work and judgmental of their employers. Before long, I noticed a change in my own spirit. I became negative and critical like those around me despite my faith in God and my positive nature. When I recognized this change, I asked God to help me to be content even in a discontented environment. Surroundings can be a source of discontentment.

A final source of discontentment is **selfishness**. An insatiable desire for personal gratification results in dissatisfaction. People are often unaware of their pursuit of personal pleasure. The search for their own advantage becomes their only source of contentment. Isn't that sad?

Do you know people who place their own interests above the welfare of others? Do you have more concern for yourself than for others? If so, you will never be content.

Jesus gave two great commandments to His children: *"You shall love the Lord your God … you shall love your neighbor as yourself"* (Matt. 22:36–39). Being content is difficult for a Christian who does not love others more than self. Contentment for the believer comes through obedience, putting others above self just as Jesus commanded.

All of us feel dissatisfied or disappointed at times. The challenge is to avoid a state of discontentment. **What is it that causes you to be unhappy? What are your sources of discontentment? As you list them below, ask God to help you avoid discontentment.**

_____

_____

_____

_____

SIGNS OF DISCONTENTMENT

Now that we have identified common sources of discontentment, let's explore some warning signs. If you truly desire to avoid unhappiness, you need to know when it's coming. Being aware of discouragement as it builds up is helpful. Often unhappiness sneaks up on us, and we are suddenly blinded by desperation and despair.

In their book, _When is Enough, Enough?_ psychotherapists Laurie Ashner and Mitch Meyerson discuss common signs of dissatisfaction. If you are thinking or asking any of the following questions, you may be headed for discontentment:

1. Why do I always feel like something is missing?
2. Why don't I follow through on my dreams?
3. Why is it that nothing makes me happy for long?
4. Why can't I just relax?
5. Why am I so bored and restless?
6. Why can't I find the right person?
7. Why do I always end up getting less than I give?
8. Why can't I stop comparing myself to other people?
9. Why do I always want the one thing I can't have?

If you feel incomplete or unfulfilled, you are susceptible to discontentment. If your happiness is fleeting or you cannot truly enjoy life, you may be discontent. If you don't feel stimulated and cannot build meaningful relationships, you are headed for disaster. If you are starving for attention or critical of your accomplishments, you will never be satisfied. If you are seeking the unobtainable or never fully satisfied, you need to learn when enough is enough. Though it is good to grow and to set goals, achieving fulfillment in life while chronically dissatisfied is impossible. As a Christian, you will miss out on God's desire for your life.

King Saul, an Old Testament leader of Israel, sought satisfaction in life. However, when he chose to disobey God's instruction to turn over his throne to David, he felt great despair. Signs of his discontentment are recorded in Scripture.

Read 1 Samuel 16:14–23. Fill in the blanks below to identify some of the signs of Saul's discontentment:

"The Spirit of the Lord _____ from Saul, and a _____ spirit from the Lord troubled him" (v. 14)

"Surely, a _____ spirit from God is troubling you" (v. 15)

"When the _____ spirit from God is upon you, and you shall be well" (v. 16)

Saul was plagued by a *distressing* spirit because God's spirit had *departed* from him. Because of his sin, Saul suffered the judgment of God and the discomfort of separation from God. God used David's talents to bring Saul back to Himself and to restore his joy. This passage concludes victoriously: *"Then Saul would become refreshed and well, and the distressing spirit would depart from him"* (v. 23). When Saul recognized his discontentment and returned to the Lord, he received satisfaction. Be aware of these signs of discontentment so you can receive His joy.

Knowing the sources and the signs of discontentment is helpful for Christians. Christians will be more motivated to avoid discontentment if they are aware of its significance. Discontentment is a powerful emotion. It has a profound effect on a person. It permeates all relationships and situations. If you are discontent, you will be affected personally, and all those around you will be influenced.

Discontentment affects all areas of life: relationship with God, relationship with others, and yourself. When you are unhappy, you have little close communion with the Lord. You spend less time in prayer and Bible study knowing the Holy Spirit will convict you of your sin. Relationships suffer. When you are dissatisfied, you tend to be critical, controlling, and crabby. In other words, you are no fun to be around. When you are discontent, your own self-worth suffers. You do not feel competent, capable, or confident. Discontentment wears a big price tag.

The book of 3 John has a good lesson about discontentment. In this short epistle, John focused on the gospel, but warned about discontentment. While God wants all His children to prosper and be content (3 John 2–4), He acknowledges the penalty for disobedience (3 John 9–11). John criticized Diotrephes, a prominent member of the church, for seeking his own way and not God's will (3 John 10). As a result, the believer Diotrephes was discontent. On the other hand, Demetrius was praised for his good testimony and his faithful obedience (3 John 12). He was content. Diotrephes paid a high price for his disobedience through discontentment. Demetrius was rewarded greatly for his obedience with contentment.

Are you aware of the significance of discontentment? Have you allowed dissatisfaction to hinder your relationship with God, others, or yourself? On the scale below, rate your personal contentment in these three relationships. Circle the number which best reflects your level of contentment.

SIGNIFICANCE OF DISCONTENTMENT

My relationship with God.

1   2   3   4   5   6   7   8   9   10
very low   very high

My relationship with others.

1   2   3   4   5   6   7   8   9   10
very low   very high

My relationship with myself.

1   2   3   4   5   6   7   8   9   10
very low   very high

One more insight from 3 John is worthy of mention. The apostle John actually acknowledged that God condones one kind of discontentment. He honors *holy discontentment*. In other words, if a believer is dissatisfied with her sinful life, or discouraged by the immorality of others, or unhappy with her own failure to obey God's will, God is pleased. God wants His children to call sin *sin,* to reject the evil ways of the world, and to follow Him faithfully every day. This is God's prescription for happiness. A believer should avoid discontentment. The only form of discontentment to be pursued by a Christian is holy discontent. Don't be satisfied with the world; be content only with Christ, our Savior and Lord.

CUSTOMIZE CONTENTMENT

If you truly desire to avoid discontentment, you must determine to do it. Develop a list of 10 Commandments for Contentment. Write them below, then put them into practice. Share these positive attitudes with others so they too can avoid discontentment.

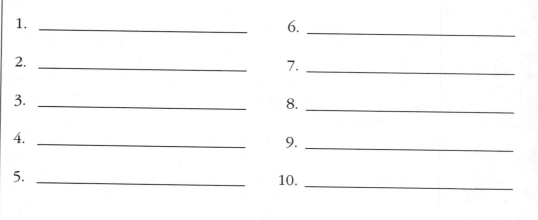

1. _____

2. _____

3. _____

4. _____

5. _____

6. _____

7. _____

8. _____

9. _____

10. _____

 ACCEPTING YOUR PAST

"Forgetting those things which are behind and reaching forward to those things which are ahead, I press toward the goal for the prize of the upward call of God in Christ Jesus" (Phil. 3:13–14).

CONTENTS FOR CONTENTMENT

Early in elementary school, students learn about parts of speech: nouns, verbs, prepositions, and so forth. Careful attention is given to verbs, those action words that must agree with the nouns. Often, verb tenses are changed to inform the reader or listener as to when the action occurred or for how long. Just as verbs have tenses—past, present, future—our relationship with God can be described in tenses. Who *were* we before Christ, who *are* we in Christ, who *will* we be in Christ?

Let's consider these descriptive tenses of salvation because they influence our state of contentment. These tenses of salvation introduce us to three important theological terms: justification, sanctification, and glorification. **Before we discuss these biblical teachings, take this brief pre-test to see what you already know about each term. Write your own understanding of these words below.**

justification _____

sanctification_____

glorification _____

The following statements summarize the basic meaning of each theological term. Think of them as the past, present, and future tenses of salvation, our ongoing relationship with Jesus Christ, the Savior of the world.

• Justification = I *was* saved from the *penalty* of sin (past tense).

• Sanctification = I *am being* saved from the *power* of sin (present tense).

• Glorification = I *will be* saved from the *presence* of sin (future tense).

When a person accepts Christ into her life, she becomes totally free from the penalty of sin and spiritual death (Rom. 3:23–25). As a believer continues growing in the likeness of Christ, she is being delivered from the power of sin over her life (1 Thess. 5:23). When the Lord returns for His children, she will be free from the presence of sin and with Him in heaven (1 Cor. 15:51–57). **Read the Scriptures noted above to better understand God's relationship with you in salvation.**

In the next three lessons, we will discover how to accept your past, present, and future. This lesson focuses on accepting your past. As you accept yourself and your circumstances throughout your life, you will be able to experience true contentment. Contentment eludes many Christians who have not come to grips with their past. Many Christians are discontent because they cannot forgive. Forgiveness is as essential to contentment as it is to salvation.

FORGIVE YOURSELF

Personal contentment cannot be experienced until each person forgives herself as God forgave her in Christ. Forgiveness is truly *"an act of God's grace to forget forever; ... the gracious human act of not holding wrong acts against a person"* (Butler, p. 509). Christians are called to practice God's forgiveness which is forgiving and forgetting. **Read the following Scriptures and affirm their teachings about forgiveness as you travel the road to contentment.**

Psalm 103:12—God's forgiveness is complete.

Jeremiah 31:34—God's forgiveness is everlasting.

1 John 1:9—God's forgiveness is available.

Is that the kind of forgiveness you received from God? Is that the kind of forgiveness you give to yourself and to others? God's forgiveness is complete, everlasting, and available. Forgiving others is often easier than forgiving ourselves. We can be our own worst critics. However, self-forgiveness is a necessary step in the pursuit of contentment. Because God has forgiven us, we are able to forgive ourselves and others.

The apostle Paul challenged the Christians in Philippi to forgive themselves and forget their past just as he himself had done. **As you read this familiar passage, think about why forgiving yourself is so important.**

"Brethren, I do not count myself to have apprehended; but one thing I do, forgetting those things which are behind and reaching forward to those things which are ahead, I press toward the goal for the prize of the upward call of God in Christ Jesus" (Phil. 3:13–14).

What are *those things which are behind* that must be forgiven? Those things could be memories of past successes or past failures. Contentment today and satisfaction tomorrow may be difficult if we fail to forget those high and low moments of life. While we can certainly learn from our mistakes and accomplishments of the past, we can also be paralyzed by them. Past failures can discourage you, and past successes may burden you. The Bible says to put the past behind you so that you can move forward now and forever. In other words, do not let your yesterday affect your today.

You cannot attain the goals God has set for you and receive His precious prizes if you do not move on. In order to move forward in the process of sanctification and the pursuit of contentment, you must forgive yourself by forgetting your past successes and past failures.

What are some things from your past that you must forgive? List them in the margin. Then put them behind.

To put these things behind, you may need to pray a prayer like David. His words recorded in Psalm 51 are paraphrased below.

Dear Lord, Please have mercy on me. Forgive my sin, wash away my impurities, and cleanse my soul. I am always aware of my sin against You, but I am also aware of Your forgiveness. So, purge my iniquities. Create in me a clean heart, O God, and renew in me my faith in You. Be present with me and empower me with Your Spirit. Restore to me the joy of Your salvation and use me to bring others to You. Then You will be pleased with my godliness. Amen.

As you acknowledge your past, confess your sin, and repent of your ways, God forgives. Out of your sorrow and despair, He gives hope. He delivers you from sin, cleanses your heart, and restores your life so you can have fellowship with Him and serve others. This process of justification will move you forward in your pursuit of contentment.

FORGIVE OTHERS

Forgiveness from God is for all, yourself and others. As God helps you forgive your own past successes and failures, you must extend forgiveness to others. That is a clear command of God and an essential ingredient for contentment. The Old Testament teaches about forgiveness through the sacrificial system. When a covenant with God or another person was broken, a sacrifice was necessary in order to restore fellowship. Forgiveness based on self-sacrifice was fleeting. In the New Testament, Jesus made the final sacrifice in His death on the cross and offered long-lasting forgiveness to all people through faith in Him.

Read Hebrews 10:1–4 and answer the following question: What does the Scripture say about sin sacrifices?

_____

_____

_____

The writer of Hebrews clearly stated that sacrificial offerings are insufficient. They must be made year by year because of the nature of sin. The Law which required sacrifices to restore broken covenants was only *"a shadow of the good things to come"* (Heb. 10:1), the ultimate sacrifice of God's Son. Christ's death on the cross provides God's forgiveness for all (Heb. 10:5–18). If you want to be content, you must accept God's forgiveness and offer it to others.

How do you forgive others? Not easily and not in your own power. You forgive others in obedience and in the power of God. No matter how serious the wrong or how repeated the sin, you are to forgive. True forgiveness is not deserved or earned but graciously given out of love. That is God's example. If you refuse to forgive, you break fellowship with your forgiving Father. If you forgive in love, you strengthen your relationship with Him.

Love is the key to forgiveness. Because God loves, He forgives. If you love God, you must forgive. Even when you are the victim, you are to forgive. Even when the other person shows no remorse, you are to forgive. Even when you do not love what a person has done or is doing, you must love the person and forgive. Forgiveness is not a feeling of love. It is an act of obedience. If you love God, you must forgive others. God supplies the love we need through the Holy Spirit in us (Rom. 15:15).

God has convinced me to forgive. When my father turned his back on God and left our family, I did not feel like loving him. I did not like what he was doing to my mother, our family, or the Lord's work; but I did love him. The Lord led me to forgive him. Before my dad asked for forgiveness, I offered it to him, because God commanded. Forgiveness strengthened my love for my dad and restored his love for the Lord. I experienced contentment in my relationship with my Heavenly Father and my earthly dad. We cannot be content if we do not forgive.

King David sang a song of praise in Psalm 32. As he reflected on the complete forgiveness of God, he was filled with joy. Because our sin has been "forgiven" (v. 1), "covered" (v. 1), and "does not impute" (v. 2), we are blessed. We can be content. Let's personalize these verses of praise: *Contented* is *she* whose transgression is forgiven, whose sin is covered. *Contented* is the *woman* to whom the Lord does not impute iniquity, and in whose spirit there is no guile.

Have you forgiven others as Christ has forgiven you? Do you need to forgive someone who has wronged you? If so, do it now. Make a phone call, make a visit, or write a letter. Ask God to help you forgive and to express your forgiveness directly to the one who has hurt you or let you down. Let God be the only judge and jury convicting people of sin. Do not be the victim. Be the victor! If you forgive, you will be content with God, yourself, and others.

FORGIVE GOD

It seems obvious that God wants us to forgive ourselves and others. It is less obvious that sometimes we may need to forgive God. God has not done anything wrong that requires forgiveness. God alone is perfect, without sin. Though forgiveness of God is not a theological truth supported by Scripture, it is a psychological reality reflected in perceptions and feelings. The children of God can be angry at Him or disappointed in His action. Thus forgiveness is necessary for fellowship. The Source of forgiveness may seem to need forgiveness in your mind.

Have you ever asked God *why?* Why did this happen? Why didn't You stop it? Christians often wonder why a God of love allows pain and suffering, why bad things happen to good people. If you are angry with God or doubting His sovereignty, you must forgive Him. *He* does not need to be forgiven. *You* need to forgive. As you forgive God, His love becomes more evident, and your relationship is restored.

Has there ever been a time when you doubted or questioned God, when you felt abandoned by Him? If so, when? How did your anger at God affect you personally?

I know someone who is angry at God. While she might not realize her feelings, they are reflected in her attitudes and actions. She continues to ask God these tough questions: *Why did you let my husband die? Where were you when my house flooded? Why did my children move away? Why is my church changing its location and worship style?* These are real questions with few real answers. In reality, God should not be held hostage by our circumstances. My friend is suffering even more because of her bitterness. Her anger at God affects her personally, and it hurts her relationship with others. She needs to forgive God and understand that He has been present with her through these life trials.

The psalmist expressed his anger at God in Psalm 73. He recognized God's goodness to others but felt personally abandoned by God. He wondered why bad things always happened to good people like him.

Read his words, written honestly and from his heart:

"But as for me, my feet had almost stumbled;
My steps had nearly slipped.
For I was envious of the boastful,
When I saw the prosperity of the wicked" (Psalm 73:1–3).

"Behold, these are the ungodly,
Who are always at ease;
They increase in riches.
Surely I have cleansed my heart in vain,
And washed my hands in innocence.
For all day long I have been plagued,
And chastened every morning" (Psalm 73:12–14).

The psalmist expressed his human emotions. He was envious of the prosperity of the wicked when he felt unrewarded in his righteousness. To him, life did not seem fair. Many Christians who have suffered feel that way. That is the feeling of my angry friend. Life is not fair! Even when life is unfair, God is always there.

If you continue reading Psalm 73, you will see that the psalmist made that discovery.

"When I thought how to understand this,
It was too painful for me
until I went into the sanctuary of God;
Then I understood their end" (Psalm 73:16–17).

"Whom have I in heaven but You?
And there is none upon earth that I desire besides You.
My flesh and my heart fail;
But God is the strength of my heart and my portion forever.
For indeed, those who are far from You shall perish;
You have destroyed all those who desert You for harlotry.
But it is good for me to draw near to God;
I have put my trust in the Lord God,
That I may declare all Your works" (Psalm 73:25–28).

My prayer for my friend is that she will forgive God as the psalmist did. In fact, that is my prayer for all Christians who are not experiencing the joy of their salvation. There is no personal contentment without deep faith. In fact, did you notice the psalmist's conclusion in verse 28? *"I have put my trust in the Lord God."* That is the key. Christians should not simply forgive God. They should trust Him. God has not wronged us. He needs no forgiveness. We have failed to depend on God, and we need to trust Him. If you trust God fully, you will be able to forgive yourself, forgive others, and forgive Him. Then you may be content. You may be happy.

CUSTOMIZE CONTENTMENT

If you truly desire to accept your past, take time to consider your blessings. Don't focus on your failures. Instead list below some past and present blessings plus future promises.

Past	**Present**	**Future**
_____	_____	_____
_____	_____	_____

Thank God for His presense, protection, and provision in your life! Now be content.

LESSON ELEVEN   ACCEPTING YOUR PRESENT

"For I know the plans that I have for you," declares the Lord, *"plans for welfare and not for calamity to give you a future and a hope."* (Jer. 29:11, NASB)

CONTENTS FOR CONTENTMENT

In this lesson, we will focus on the present tense of our relationship with Jesus Christ, the process of sanctification. The only way for a Christian to be truly content right now is to be actively growing in the Lord. That is the process of sanctification, *"being made holy resulting in a changed lifestyle for the believer"* (Butler, p. 1230). Thus, the believer's lifetime should be spent seeking to be like Christ. Though humans can never achieve His level of perfection, there is great contentment in becoming more like Him.

How can you accept your present? How can you be completely satisfied with the life you are now living? In the same way that justification is dependent on the power of God, sanctification is also dependent on God alone. The believer attempts to lead a godly life, but only God can empower the believer to be holy.

Contentment in your life is totally dependent on the power and the presence of God. The presence of God will bring about change in your life and help you accept your present.

As we consider the role of the Holy Spirit in your life, evaluate your present. Answer the questions below:

Who are you? _____

What are you doing? _____

How do you sense God's presence? _____

God and God alone identifies who you are. You are created in the image of God (Gen. 1:27); you are equal in the eyes of God (Gal. 3:28); you are worthy (2 Thess. 1:5); you are loved (Rom 8:39); you are His (Eph. 2:19). Those affirmations alone can give you cause for contentment. Your activity should also be defined by Him. God says that the work you are doing is important. You are serving as His ambassador (2 Cor. 5:20); you are accomplishing His purpose (Rom. 8:28, 30); you are His hands and feet (Isa. 52:7); you are investing your life in the lives of others (2 Cor. 3:2–3); your efforts for Him make an eternal difference (Heb. 12:1–2). Your identity in Him and your work for Him should be enough to satisfy your soul, but God also gives you His presence. He is with you from the time of your salvation and throughout all eternity to enable you to accomplish His work and to give you abundant life. God is present with you through the Holy Spirit.

The Holy Spirit is the third Person of the Trinity. One way to understand God is to understand how He relates to His children. That special relationship is expressed in three ways. The *Father* is God ruling over us in creation; the *Son* is God acting for our salvation; and the *Spirit* is God dwelling in us to help us live a holy life. Let's open the Scripture to understand how to be content in God's presence, content in God's plan, and content in God's provision. The only way to be truly satisfied in life is to be content in His presence.

CONTENT IN HIS PRESENCE

My Grandfather Harrington taught me a profound lesson about practicing the presence of God just a few years before his death. While eating at his favorite restaurant, we sat at a table for four even though there were just two of us. He explained that when he ate there, he always sat at a table for four because he was not alone. There were chairs for his wife, his mother, and the Holy Spirit. Though they were not physically present, he sensed their presence with him. He was practicing the presence of God! I have never forgotten that lesson. Now I try to practice His presence all the time. (By the way, my granddaddy warned me about talking out loud to God in public!)

The Bible teaches that God has always been present and will always be present. His presence is one thing we can count on. What a promise! God is not simply present in the world. He is present in relationships. **Read the following accounts and note how each person sensed God's presence.**

Passage	Person	God's Presence
Exodus 3:1–22		
Exodus 19:3–6		
1 Kings 19:12–13		
Isaiah 6:1–8		
Acts 9:1–9		

God has often revealed Himself clearly to man through His presence. Through a burning bush, God spoke to Moses about his role in leading the Israelites out of Egypt (Ex. 3:1–22). Later, God appeared again to Moses with a message for the children of Israel (Ex. 19:3–6). The Lord visited the prophet Isaiah in the Jerusalem Temple. God extended a call to Isaiah to be a prophet, and He proclaimed His holiness through the seraphim (Isa. 6:1–8). In the New Testament, Paul encountered the Lord on the Damascus Road. It was there, in God's presence, that Paul was converted and began spreading the gospel (Acts 9:1–9). Sometimes God's presence is revealed physically, but always God's presence is experienced personally by the believer.

Has there ever been a time when you have truly experienced the presence of God? Describe that encounter here and explain how God's presence strengthened your faith.

Whether you experience a dramatic encounter with the Lord as Paul did on the Damascus Road or you are aware of His presence through His still, small voice, you can be assured that God is present with you. He is with you. He is going before you. He is carrying you. God's presence is a comfort, a guide, and a shield for believers at all times.

CONTENT IN HIS PLAN

There is certainly cause for contentment as a believer experiences the presence of God. There is also contentment in knowing and doing His will. **Are you content in God's plan?** One of the Christian's greatest life challenges is understanding what God intends for her to do. God attempts to make His will clear to us throughout the different stages of life. Once God's plan is known, the believer must choose to obey God and follow His plan. In obedience and in faithfulness, there is true contentment.

A key passage about the will of God was written by the prophet Isaiah. God Himself assured the children of Israel that He did have a plan for them and that His plan was perfect At a time when they did not know what to do or where to go, God spoke to them clearly. **Read the passage below and then personalize God's message for you in your own words in the space below.**

"'For I know the plans that I have for you,' declares the Lord, 'plans for welfare and not for calamity to give you a future and a hope.

'Then you will call upon Me and come and pray to Me, and I will listen to you.

'And you will seek Me and find Me, when you search for Me with all your heart'" (Jer. 29:11–13 NASB).

_____

_____

_____

God assured the Israelites and He assures His children today that He does have a plan for each one of us. His plan is *definite*. His plan is also for our good. It should be *desired*. His plan for our lives will bring greater

71

blessing than we can imagine, but we must seek His will, *discover* it. If you want to be content, you must know and do God's will.

Reread the verses above from Jeremiah 29. Did you notice some conditions to His promised plan? What must the Christian do in order to be led by God? Fill in the blanks below to complete the phrases from Scripture which prescribe our action.

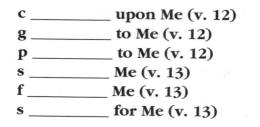

c _____ upon Me (v. 12)
g _____ to Me (v. 12)
p _____ to Me (v. 12)
s _____ Me (v. 13)
f _____ Me (v. 13)
s _____ for Me (v. 13)

Only when you *call* on God, *go* to Him, *pray* to Him, *seek* Him, *find* Him, and *search* for Him with all your heart will you truly know the plans God has for you. Then you can be content in His plans.

Whenever I faced major life decisions, I meditated on Jeremiah 29:11–13. Whether it was a decision about which college to attend or what major to study, who to marry or where to live, where to work or how to minister, I could be confident in God's plan for me. Even now as I make decisions about what to do with my life, I diligently call on God. I search for His will with all of my heart. As I discover and do His will, I am content in my obedience and His plan. These are other Scriptures that encourage me as I seek God's plan for my life.

Romans 12:1, 2— *"I beseech you therefore, brethren, by the mercies of God, that you present your bodies a living sacrifice, holy, acceptable to God, which is your reasonable service. And do not be conformed to this world, but be transformed by the renewing of your mind, that you may prove what is the good and acceptable and perfect will of God."*

Philippians 1:6— *"Being confident of this very thing, that He who has begun a good work in you will complete it until the day of Jesus Christ."*

Colossians 1:9, 10— *"For this reason we also, since the day we heard it, do not cease to pray for you, and to ask that you may be filled with the knowledge of His will in all wisdom and spiritual understanding; that you may have a walk worthy of the Lord, fully pleasing Him, being fruitful in every good work and increasing in the knowledge of God."*

I pray that you will be confident in knowing God's plan and contented in doing it.

True contentment is found in the presence of God and in His plan for your life. We encounter deep satisfaction in His protection. In a world filled with violence and hatred, knowing that God will take care of His children is comforting. In a life facing fears and uncertainty, knowing that God protects is reassuring. God's arms of love reach out to you, and His wings of strength cover you in concern. You can sleep. You can rest knowing that God is watching over you. Ahh, that is cause for contentment.

The psalmist wrote of the safety of the Almighty's arms. **Read Psalm 91. Identify several visual images that help you understand the protective love of God. Write your thoughts in the margin.**

CONTENT IN HIS PLAN

You can totally trust God to protect you. You can be secure in Him because His presence covers you (v. 1). He is your refuge or shelter, your fortress or strong tower (v. 2). He delivers you from danger and protects you from disease (v. 3). He guards His young children and gives courage to the fearful (v. 4). There is absolutely nothing that can compare to the security God provides His children. We can be content in His care!

Have you ever been afraid? Can you remember a time when you were gripped with fear? Remember that experience here.

———————————————————————————

———————————————————————————

Fear is a common emotion even for a believer. Some people are afraid of speaking in front of large groups or afraid of snakes. Others fear failure or rejection. Any fear is real. It is very real to the one facing it. The Christian can be reassured by the presence and protection of God.

Several years ago I began to fear flying. That is a disruptive fear for a frequent flyer. My fear developed through a series of bumpy flights. I feared things out of my control: the weather, piloting a plane, motion sickness. During that time, God used an article written by Jill Briscoe to remind me of God's protection even at 30,000 feet in the air. She had experienced fear of flying, too, but God convicted her of the incongruity of fear and faith. If a believer has deep faith, experiencing fear should be difficult because of God's promises to protect. Jill Briscoe concluded: *"When I couldn't feel Him with my feelings, I decided that day somewhere over the Midwest, I would seek Him with my faith. I decided not to be afraid... Fear and faith cannot live together"* (Virtue, p. 68). I made that decision too. I chose faith, not fear. I memorized a Scripture that assures me of God's protection whenever fear creeps in: *"Fear not, for I am with you; be not dismayed, for I am your God"* (Isa. 41:10).

Let me share one other personal struggle for contentment. While writing this Bible study, I have faced my first personal health problem. I have always been in excellent health and full of energy. This health crisis has been particularly challenging. Fulfilling responsibilities and maintaining focus while the doctors try to diagnose my problem has been hard. The symptoms persist, and the treatments seem unsuccessful. So I must put my trust in God daily. I must trust Him with my life and my health. While honestly, I don't *feel* like it, I must choose to be content in the present. I can do so because of my knowledge of *His* presence, of *His* plan, and of my experience of *His* protection.

Contentment in the present does not preclude forgiveness of the past or planning for the future. It does mean choosing peace and satisfaction in the moment. As you take personal responsibility for the past and the future, you can truly be free to enjoy the present. The present moment is the only time you may have. So choose to use it wisely. The believer can be content in the present because of God's presence, God's plan, and God's protection. He is our only source of contentment.

CUSTOMIZE CONTENTMENT

Carefuly read and meditate on Jeremiah 29:11. What do you think are the plans God has for you? _____

What are you doing to seek His will? _____

Voice a prayer of commitment to God to seek and follow His plan.

 ESSON TWELVE  ACCEPTING YOUR FUTURE

"We do not look at the things which are seen, but at the things which are not seen. For the things which are seen are temporary, but the things which are not seen are eternal"
(2 Cor. 4:18).

The believer is admonished in Scripture to accept life with its past problems, present challenges, and future uncertainties. However, being satisfied when life brings disappointments and pain is hard. There is hope, hope in the Lord and hope for the future. A believer must continually strive to achieve contentment.

Contentment is dependent upon acceptance of past successes and failures, acceptance of present trials and victories, and acceptance of future mysteries and unknowns. The future for a Christian includes the process of glorification, actually being in the presence of God for all eternity. At that time, we will experience eternal contentment, no longer in the presence of sin or sorrow.

Think for a few minutes about your future, your time left here on earth and your eternity with God in heaven. How do you feel about your future? What do you anticipate and what do you dread? Honestly write your feelings here.

_____

_____

Feeling some concern about the future is not at all wrong for the Christian. Though you may have complete confidence in God, you may still feel anxious about the uncertainties of the future. Questioning the unknown and dreading the undesired is natural. No one wants to experience pain, suffering, death, or loss; but those life experiences are probable. God's Word answers the Christian's questions, and God's sovereignty can allay our doubts.

Take time to meditate on these Scriptures that assure us of a future hope despite the uncertainties of tomorrow.

"Behold, the eye of the Lord is on those who fear Him, on those who hope in His mercy, to deliver their soul from death, and to keep them alive in famine" (Psalm 33: 18–19).

"Do not let your heart envy sinners, but be zealous for the fear of the Lord all day; For surely there is a hereafter, and your hope will not be cut off" (Prov. 23:17–18).

"For the grace of God that brings salvation has appeared to all men, teaching us that, denying ungodliness and worldly lusts, we should live soberly, righteously, and godly in the present age, looking for the blessed hope and glorious appearing of our great God and Savior Jesus Christ" (Titus 2:11–13).

"This hope we have as an anchor of the soul, both sure and steadfast, and which enters the Presence behind the veil" (Heb. 6:19).

Share these words of assurance with other believers.

There are many reasons for Christians to have hope even in the midst of present trials and future uncertainties. There is hope in God the Father who has a plan and purpose for each life plus the power to conquer all. There is hope in Christ the Son. His death on the cross provides salvation, and His resurrection from the dead defeats the power of sin and death. There is also hope in the Holy Spirit whose presence strengthens the believer and gives guidance. Christians can live with confidence in the present and courage in the future because of God. That is cause for contentment and a reason for glory.

Let's discuss *glory* and *glorification*. *Glorification* comes when the believer enters the presence of God in heaven. *Glory* is what the believer can experience right here on earth. Glory means *"to praise, to recognize the importance of another"* (Butler, p. 557). As a Christian understands who God is, she realizes He alone is worthy to be praised. As a believer sees God at work, she acknowledges Him through worship. As a believer seeks God's will, she follows Him in obedience. Glory is a believer's work of worship until she is glorified for all eternity. God is worthy of our glory, and our expressions of glory can help us develop contentment. Express your contentment as you glory in the unknown, in the mysterious, and in the eternal.

GLORY IN THE UNKNOWN

God is to be praised even when life is uncertain and the future is unknown. Glorifying the Lord when life is joyful and prayers are answered is easy. Praising the Lord in tough times and while waiting on Him is difficult. Remember that God is worthy of our praise at all times. You may realize that often praise is a prelude to contentment. Our praise, which begins in obedience, may lead to contentment. God is worthy of glory even in the unknown.

The Christian faces many unknowns. That is why one must have faith. Faith alone gives hope and explains the unknown. Hebrews 11:1 reminds us, *"faith is the substance of things hoped for, the evidence of things not seen."* If you have faith, you can glory in the unknown. Paul said it this way: *"We do not look at the things which are seen, but at things which are not seen. For the things which are seen are temporary, but the things which are not seen are eternal"* (2 Cor. 4:18). It is the things which are known only to God that should matter to the believer.

Read 2 Corinthians 4:18 in several different translations of the Bible. Underline some key words and phrases in the verse then try to understand it by faith. Write a paraphrase of that verse in your own words.

_____

_____

_____

_____

Will your faith be strong as you face the uncertainties of the future? Death is a great unknown. Can you face death with great faith? There is one certainty about death. It is certain. While death is inevitable, the details are unknown. The Bible addresses the topic of death throughout its pages. It clearly states that everyone who lives will die: *"To everything there is a season, ... a time to be born, and a time to die"* (Eccl. 3:1–2). The Bible verifies that life is short and should be lived to the fullest: *"For what is your life? It is even a vapor that appears for a little time and then vanishes away"* (James 4:14). The Bible warns that death is followed by judgment: *"God will bring every work into judgment, including every secret thing, whether good or evil"* (Eccl. 12:14). Christians must accept death, live life, and prepare for judgment. That should keep us busy and should give us hope.

My father-in-law was in the funeral business for more than 40 years. He faithfully ministered to families during their times of loss. He once talked about comforting others in grief. He had astutely observed that even Christians had difficulty finding words to convey their feelings of sorrow. Understandably, speaking when you don't know what to say is hard. Death is so final and grief is so great that words seem trite. I will never forget his counsel to me: "Even when you don't know what to say, say something." Speak words of love and comfort to a grieving friend. Give words of hope and confidence in the Lord to believers facing loss. Though death is painful, there is joy in the future hope.

Christians must glory in the unknown. It is impossible to be content in life if you cannot praise God who helps you face the uncertainties of the future. While death means an end to this physical life, death for the believer also begins everlasting life in the presence of God. That is the time we experience glorification. That is reason to praise God, to glory in the unknown and even in the mysterious.

GLORY IN THE MYSTERIOUS

Because of Christ, Christians can glory in the unknown and even the mysterious. There are many mysteries in life, things that cannot be understood by the human mind. We should not be surprised that there are things about God that we do not understand. After all, He is God, and we are not. It is natural to wonder and to be curious. A part of our spiritual growth should be increased knowledge. So how does the Christian accept by faith things not understood and actually glory in the mysterious? That is a real tension of the Christian life.

The Bible speaks a lot about mysteries.

Read the following passages then identify the particular mystery mentioned.

Matthew 13:11 _____

Mark 4:11 _____

1 Corinthians 2:7–8 _____

Ephesians 3:3–5 _____

Colossians 2:2 _____

The New Testament uses the word _mystery_ about 25 times referring to _"matters previously kept secret in God's eternal purposes"_ (Butler, p. 998). It speaks of the _"mysteries of the kingdom of heaven"_ (Matt. 13:11), _"the mystery of the kingdom of God"_ (Mark 4:11), _"the wisdom of God in a mystery"_ (1 Cor. 2:7–8), _"the mystery of Christ"_ (Eph. 3:3–5), and _"the knowledge of the mystery of God"_ (Col. 2:2). The mysteries of God are spiritual and relate to the gospel message of Jesus Christ. As we grow in the Lord, some of His mysteries are revealed. There will always be mysteries about God because of His infinite and divine knowledge. In fact, we should be glad for the mysteries since our human mind cannot comprehend His thoughts.

God's grace is the greatest mystery. How can God love us so much that He sent His Son to die for us on the cross to provide our salvation? That is a mystery filled with glory. **What are some of the mysteries of God that you do not understand?**

_____

_____

_____

Each believer faces confusion about God, but our faith can still be strong. While mystery concerning the end times and curiosity

about heaven has always been around, more interest in these seems evident today than ever before. The overwhelming response to the *Left Behind* Series by Tim LaHaye and Jerry Jenkins is a striking example of the search for truth. These popular novels, based on Scripture, have topped the best-seller lists even in the secular market. Why? Because of the mystery. Is it not encouraging to see an openness to God and His Word through the curiosity of the human mind?

Though we will never fully understand, the Bible does speak clearly about the end times. There is a theological field of eschatology, *"the study of last things or the events that are awaiting future fulfillment"* (*The Woman's Study Bible*, p. 1997). While theologians may differ in their views and many details are unclear, the Bible confirms numerous facts about the end times: Jesus Christ will return; He will reign on earth; everyone will be judged; and everyone will spend eternity in heaven or hell. (See the following key Scripture passages: Matt. 24:36–44; 1 Cor. 15:50–57; 1 Thess. 4:13–18; Rev. 19:1–22:5.) The Bible gives us one command regarding the end times: *"Be ready"* (Matt. 24:44). Since we don't know exactly when or how Christ will return, believers must be ready at all times. We can glory in that mystery.

There is mystery about heaven. While believers discuss "the streets of gold" and long for "no more pain," much about heaven is unknown. Where is it? What will it actually look like? Will we know each other? Will there be marriages in heaven? These are mysteries, but the Bible does tell us that God has prepared heaven for us (John 14:1–3) and that there will be no sorrow or sin (Rev. 21:1–7). The most important truth about heaven is the presence of God. Believers will be with Him forever. This biblical teaching about heaven is a fundamental doctrine of the faith. (To learn more about heaven, I recommend the Bible study *Heaven: Your Real Home* by Joni Eareckson Tada.) Don't let questions about heaven rob you of the joy of faith. Glory in the mysteries.

GLORY IN THE ETERNAL

Believers should glory in the unknown and glory in the mysteries, but we can truly praise God for the eternal. Has it fully dawned on you what eternity is all about? Eternity is forever. Eternity is defined as *"a seemingly endless, immeasurable time."* The believer is promised eternal life, life without end in the presence of God. Eternity includes both unlimited length of life and unsurpassed quality of life. If you believe that biblical truth, then you can glory in the eternal.

One of the most significant attributes of God is His eternal nature. God has no beginning and no end; He existed before time and creation (Psalm 90:2). God is concerned with time though time has no hold on Him (Psalm 90:4–6). He is continually present with us as the Sovereign Lord of creation. When an individual comes to faith in Jesus Christ, eternal life is received. From the point of salvation, the believer begins to live eternally.

Though physical death will come to all people, spiritual life continues for believers throughout eternity.

Read the following Scriptures. Then state your understanding of eternal life promised to believers: John 3:15–16; John 3:36; John 10:28; and John 17:3.

_____

_____

_____

There is a past, a present and a future tense of eternity. God has been at work in the world for all eternity. That is eternity past (Psalm 90:1–2). Personally, you began to live eternally in the past when you accepted Christ as your Savior. Now God is at work in the present bringing others to eternal life. You are experiencing eternal life in the present as you live for God and walk in His Spirit. In the future, God will reign forever, and You will fellowship with Him for all eternity (John 5:24).

The apostle John wrote extensively about eternal life. The theme of eternity was also repeated in the other gospels and in Paul's epistles. Eternal life is essential to a believer's understanding of salvation. Eternal life is a promise that gives great hope and promotes praise to God.

Read what Jesus Himself said about eternal life in John 5:24–30.

"Most assuredly, I say to you, he who hears My word and believes in Him who sent Me has everlasting life, and shall not come into judgment, but has passed from death into life. Most assuredly, I say to you, the hour is coming, and now is, when the dead will hear the voice of the Son of God; and those who hear will live. For as the Father has life in Himself, so He has granted the Son to have life in Himself, and has given Him authority to execute judgment also, because He is the Son of Man. Do not marvel at this; for the hour is coming in which all who are in the graves will hear His voice and come forth—those who have done good, to the resurrection of life, and those who have done evil, to the resurrection of condemnation. I can of Myself do nothing. As I hear, I judge; and My judgment is righteous, because I do not seek My own will but the will of the Father who sent Me."

You may also want to read what the apostle says about eternal life in John 14.

Christians today have many reasons to be content. We can rejoice even in the unknown, the mysterious, and the eternal because of God's promises to protect us, provide for us, and be present with us. As we rejoice, we bring glory to God. Our glory to God honors Him and leads others to Him. In your homes, in your businesses, in your churches, and in your communities, you can glorify God. Your praise of Him is a powerful witness.

Truett Cathey, the successful Christian businessman, has made glorifying God the primary vision of his life and work. When he established his international restaurant chain Chick-fil-A, Mr. Cathey determined to put God first. His restaurants are closed on Sundays so that his employees can attend worship services. He developed a purpose statement that focuses on God: *"Our corporate purpose: To glorify God by being a faithful steward of all that is entrusted to us"* (*Focus on the Family,* September 2000, pp. 2–4). What a testimony to God! What a witness in the business world! Mr. Cathey was willing to risk economic loss in order to glorify God.

That is our challenge today. Will your faith in God be strong enough that you can trust Him with your future? Though there are unknowns and mysteries which will last for all eternity, you can be confident in our eternal, all-knowing God. He can give you true contentment if you accept your past, your present, and your future.

As you face the future with its unknowns and mysteries, you can be confident in God who is present with you for all eternity. In the space below, write a prayer of commitment expressing your desire to follow God all the days of your life and your hope of an eternity with Him.

CUSTOMIZE CONTENTMENT

_____

_____

_____

_____

_____

Your commitment to Him should give you great contentment!

CONCLUSION—CONTENT IN HIS CARE

Our Bible study on personal contentment is coming to an end. We have examined contentment from all angles: what it is, where it comes from, and how we get it. We have studied the Scriptures to understand how to accept God, ourselves, others, and our circumstances. We have identified ways to avoid discontentment by turning away from negative thoughts and feelings that rob our joy. We have looked behind us, around us, and ahead of us to know the past, the present, and the future tenses of contentment. The most important question still to be asked is: Are you content?

I challenge you to fill out the Contentment Questionnaire Post-test. Find out if your thoughts on contentment have changed since participating in this study. I predict that they have. You may, after having examined who your contentment is based on and who you are in Him, have a higher level of contentment. If so, continue to focus on Him. On the other hand, you may have a lower level of contentment because you now have a deeper understanding of what contentment is and have come to recognize areas of discontentment in your life that you did not realize were there. If so, my advice is the same, focus on Him. Give these areas of discontentment to Him and commit to contentment.

A current women's magazine included "The Happiness Report" (*Good Housekeeping*, September 2000). Researchers in the new field of well-being psychology concluded that *"our happiness depends on surprisingly trivial and often changeable things"* such as money, beauty, youth, brains, or good weather. Further they concluded that *"we may be looking for joy in all the wrong places."* That should not surprise Christians. The world seems to be fruitless in its search for joy. We see our friends seeking happiness in relationships or success in their work. Even Christians are prone to overlook the obvious Source of satisfaction when life's circumstances get stressful. Are you guilty of envy or despair? Have you ever had a pity party? Do your moods vacillate? Well, let's stop that cycle of discontent and be content in His care.

Christians should be content. Christians should be satisfied with life. Christians should spread His joy to others. If you experience only fleeting moments of happiness and lack true joy, let me suggest a few more strategies for your search to find personal contentment. Do not settle for moments of glee. Seek a lifetime of true contentment. Try a mental exercise to start this process.

Imagine yourself on a secluded beach with silky sand, relaxing surf, cool breeze, fragrant flowers, and no hassles. Who could not be content in that setting? If you are not a beach person, imagine yourself in the mountains or in the desert, but situated in a fantasy land. Our great challenge in life is to be content in all circumstances and all settings. We can achieve contentment when we realize *whose* we are, not *where* we are. God, who created the beautiful places in the world, is in control of the chaos in your life. Even in the storms of life, you can be calm and content. How?

An important truth for Christians is that you can be content because you are in God's care! Do you believe that? I pray you do. If not, you need the contentment that is possible through His grace. If so, you need to *savor* your contentment, *store* up your contentment, and *share* your contentment.

Think back to the beach or to the mountains or to the desert. You can continue to experience the joy of that setting if you savor it, store it up, and share it. Even back at home, you can remember the sights, smells, and sounds of the beach. Ahhh, savor the moment! When you return home, you can start planning your next vacation or get-away. You can store up more refreshing memories. You can share your experience with others through your words, photographs, and journal. Though we may never get to our fantasy island, we will one day get to heaven. What a great day that will be! Remember that day is closer now than ever before.

Chuck and I love to travel. We have learned a lot in our travels, not just from the places we have visited but in the process of traveling itself. One lesson I learned is how to pack for a trip. First you stack; then you sack; then you pack. As a big trip approaches, I start pulling out things to take. I stack them. Then I begin buying needed articles. I sack them. Just before we leave, I actually pack everything in the suitcase. That's a practical lesson. I have also learned a philosophical lesson about travel. Every trip has three stages: planning the trip, taking the trip, and remembering the trip. I truly enjoy each stage. That is why travel is such fun. That may help us as Christians learn how to be content.

If we savor His care, store up His care, and share His care, we can truly be content. In fact, only then can we experience a lifetime of

84

contentment and an eternity of His care. It is my prayer that you will make a lifetime commitment to be content. Contentment in Christ will be a blessing to you and a witness to others.

1. I am content...   1   2   3   4   5

          seldom if ever   sometimes   always

Why? _____

_____

_____

Why not? _____

2. What do you understand contentment to be? _____

_____

3. What causes you to be content? _____

_____

4. What causes you to be discontent? _____

_____

5. How do you seek contentment? _____

_____

6. Describe the contentment level of your spouse (if married). _____

_____

Comments: _____

_____

_____

_____

_____

GROUP TEACHING GUIDE

You may want to have an introductory session in which you introduce the study, distribute books, review the format of the book, and get to know the women in your group. Some groups may not have that opportunity and will need to start immediately with Lesson One as described here. Adapt these teaching suggestions accordingly. If your group members were not able to prepare lesson one, you will need to teach its contents before the discussion.

LESSON ONE

Prayer Time (5 minutes)
Ask each member of the group to write a commitment to complete this Bible study on contentment. Encourage her to write it in the front of her book. Then spend a few minutes in prayer asking God to bless this study.

Introduction (5 minutes)
Discuss the format for this study and details about the group meeting. Ask each member to try to complete her own personal study before discussing it with the group.

Digesting Contents for Contentment (5 minutes)
Work on memorizing 1 Timothy 6:6 together. Form pairs and ask the women to say the verse to each other seven times, emphasizing a different word each time. Then invite them to share with each other one way that godliness with contentment is great gain. When the pairs return to the large group, lead everyone in saying the verse together.

Group Discussion (40 minutes)
Lead the group to share and discuss their responses to the contentment questionnaire. If your group just received their books, allow women time to complete the questionnaire before the discussion. Tell women that they will have another chance to complete the questionnaire at the end of the study.

Ask group members to share their definitions of contentment. Develop a group definition based on the contents of the lesson and group input. Write this definition on a large sheet of paper and post it during each group meeting. Note for the group that it may be revised as you continue the study.

Call on volunteers to read the Scriptures regarding acceptance. Discuss the Bible's teaching about acceptance. Pose the question, "What is the key to sincere acceptance?" Ask members to share how contentment leads to action. Ask, "What parts do obedience and God's sovereignty play in this?"

Read the passages in Ecclesiastes. Trace the development of King Solomon's attitude. Ask: "What was Solomon's attitude in the final passage? How did he arrive at this attitude?"

Closing (5 minutes)
Close by reading aloud together the words of the chorus of "We Follow the Lord" as a prayer of commitment.

LESSON TWO

Prayer Time (5 minutes)
Open with a time of conversational prayer, praising God for who He is. Encourage members to use the names and attributes of God in their prayers.

Review (5 minutes)
Read your group definition of contentment. Ask if group members want to make changes in the definition. Ask if they have become aware of what contentment is in their daily lives.

Digesting Contents for Contentment (5 minutes)
Read Deuteronomy 4:39 aloud. Ask the following questions to elicit replies directly from the verse:

Q: Who is God?   **A:** The Lord Himself.
Q: Where is He God?   **A:** In heaven and on the earth .
Q: Who else is God?   **A:** There is no other.

Read the verse together again.

Group Discussion (40 minutes)
Discuss what God's sovereignty means to each person. Ask, "How can God relate to you in authority and in love?" Compare and contrast these attributes of God: *omnipotence, omniscience,* and *omnipresence.* Use the Scriptures and the Bible study to gather insights. Invite group

members to mention some unpleasant changes in life. Discuss God's unchanging character. Thank God for His immutability.

Discuss the true-false statements at the end of the lesson. Summarize the nature of God.

Closing (5 minutes)
As you conclude, encourage members to write prayers of praise, thanking God for who He is to them and to the universe. Ask one member to close the prayer time.

Prayer Time (5 minutes)
Ask group members to pair up with other group members for prayer. Thank God for who He made you to be. Encourage members to thank God for specific characteristics He gave them, such as looks, talents, and even weaknesses.

Review (5 minutes)
Review your definition of contentment and ask if members want to make changes. Ask, "Who does our contentment come from?" Encourage members to share characteristics of God that lead to contentment.

Digesting Contents for Contentment (5 minutes)
Read 1 Peter 2:9 leaving out the last word in each descriptive phrase and allowing the group to supply it. Next, form pairs and ask one partner read the verse as you did while the other partner supplies the missing word. Let partners switch roles. Read the verse is this manner:

reader: **You are a chosen**   other: **generation**
reader: **a royal**   other: **priesthood**
reader: **a holy**   other: **nation**
reader: **His own**   other: **special people**
reader: **1 Peter**   other: **2:9**

Repeat the verse as a group.

Group Discussion (40 minutes)
Summarize the story of Moses. Ask group members whether or not they think Moses was truly content. Remind them of Leviticus 10:20.

Ask members to underline in 1 Peter 2:9 four key words: *chosen, royal, holy, special.* Discuss how each word can help a believer accept who she is.

Allow time for members to reflect on their holiness scales. Direct a time of silent prayer during which members may seek God's forgiveness for their unholiness and ask for His help in developing holiness.

Distribute paper. Urge members to write notes of appreciation to people special to them. Encourage them to mail the notes. Stress developing close relationships with other people.

Closing (5 minutes)
Close with sentence prayers in the group. Ask members to voice one sentence affirming another group member's worth and value. Mention each lady by name during the prayer time.

LESSON FOUR

Prayer Time (5 minutes)
Open with prayer, thanking God for the group's spiritual gifts. As you thank Him, remember the many ways those gifts are expressed in ministry to others.

Review (5 minutes)
Review some of the words from 1 Peter 2:9 that describe who you are—*chosen, royal, holy, special.* Ask members if they have experienced more contentment in who they are during the past week.

Digesting Contents for Contentment (5 minutes)
Read 1 Peter 4:10. Ask the class to list characteristics of gifts based on this verse. Characteristics should include that each believer has received one, that we are to minister it to one another as good stewards, and that it comes by the grace of God.

Group Discussion (40 minutes)
Ask the group to share favorite gifts they have received. As a gift is mentioned, let the person explain why it was special.

Call for volunteers to read their definitions of spiritual gifts. Review the definitions from the Bible study to enhance understanding of spiritual gifts.

Pose the following questions for clarification: "Who is the giver of all spiritual gifts? (God) Who is the recipient of spiritual gifts? (every believer)"

Assign each of these six key passages to a different individual or to a small group: *Romans 12:6–8; 1 Corinthians 12:8–10; 1 Corinthians 12:28–30; 1 Corinthians 13:1–3; Ephesians 4:11–16; 1 Peter 4:9–10..*

Ask each individual or group to list the spiritual gifts identified in its passage. After a few minutes, call for reports and compile a master list on a board or poster.

Discuss the difference between spiritual gifts and natural talents. Ask members to share examples of people who have turned talents into gifts of ministry.

Closing (5 minutes)
Encourage group members to reflect on the spiritual gifts and the plan for ministry noted in Customize Contentment. Close with a prayer of commitment to use the gifts God has given for His glory.

Prayer Time (5 minutes)
Ask group members to write the names of their family members including both immediate and extended family. Spend time praying silently for specific family members.

Review (5 minutes)
Review basic facts about spiritual gifts. Ask, "Have you seen believers this past week use their spiritual gifts to minister to others?"

Digesting Contents for Contentment (5 minutes)
Read together Hebrews 13:5. Suggest words that could replace content and still have the same meaning. Possibilities are *satisfied*, *happy*, or *grateful*. Repeat the verse together again.

Group Discussion (40 minutes)
Read Ephesians 5:22–33 aloud. Let members write on a poster or a board words to describe their understandings of biblical relationships under these headings: *Christ–Church* and *Husband–Wife*.

Suggest group members spend a few minutes talking to other group members about their extended families. Encourage them to show pictures and get to know each other's families. Be sensitive to the women who have no children and let them tell of nieces, nephews, or other child relatives.

Discuss ways group members can build extended family relationships. Mention specifically holiday family times.

Ask members to describe their dream houses. Encourage women to focus on what makes a loving home rather than a beautiful house. Challenge women to be content with their houses while building stronger homes.

LESSON SIX

Closing (5 minutes)

Provide a blank 3-by-5-inch card for each group member. Ask members to write on the cards specific prayer requests for family members. Guide ladies to exchange cards and pray for each other's families. Take the cards home and continue praying for the request.

Prayer Time (5 minutes)

Divide the group into prayer triplets, three women praying together. Ask groups to praise God for His gracious provision. Then ask women to share financial needs with each other, either personal needs, needs of others, needs of the church or needs of other ministries. Pray specifically for these financial needs.

Review (5 minutes)

Review the section in Lesson Five titled "Accepting Your Family." Call for volunteers who can recall names of other members' immediate family. Ask ladies to share family updates.

Digesting Contents for Contentment (5 minutes)

Ask each group member to read one word of the focal passage, 1 Timothy 6:8. For a small group, keep going around the group until the verse is complete. For a large group, continue repeating the verse until each lady has participated. Ask: Are you content when your basic needs are met?

Group Discussion (40 minutes)

Discuss the meaning and purpose of parables in Scripture. Assign these five parables to different individuals or to small groups: *Matthew 13:45–46; Matthew 25:14–30; Luke 12:13–21; Luke 15:8–10; and Luke 16:1–13*. Ask groups or individuals to read their parables and then report to the group the spiritual truths learned.

Review the true-false questions about God's provision. Read 1 Timothy 6:6-10 to identify the correct answers.

Ask group members to picture greed. Ask, "What does greed look like?" Use a board or a large sheet of paper to let members draw a greedy woman. For example, a woman may be dressed beautifully, but her face would be unhappy or even angry.

Call for two volunteers to read 1 Timothy 6:6–10. Suggest that they alternate reading the verses, one reading verses 6, 8, and 10 and the other reading verses 7 and 9. As a group, discuss the biblical warnings about the love of money.

Allow members to complete the personal inventory of material possessions. Encourage them to set specific goals and priorities for letting go of things in order to simplify their lives and help them be content.

Closing (5 minutes)

Ask each group member to find a Scriptures in this lesson that is a promise of God's provision. Invite each one to pray that Scripture silently. Pause a women pray. Close with your own spoken prayer.

Prayer Time (5 minutes)

Read James 1:2–4 aloud as group members meditate on the passage. Ask women to pray silently about facing trials. Close the prayer time thanking God aloud for His strength during our trials.

Review (5 minutes)

Review the biblical teachings about finances found in 1 Timothy 6:6–10. Ask members to share what God has been teaching them about accepting their finances.

Digesting Contents for Contentment (5 minutes)

Invite group members to read Philippians 4:11 silently except that as each person comes to the word whatever she will say that word aloud. Briefly mention some whatever states in which we must be content.

Group Discussion (40 minutes)

Refer group members to the Chuck Kelley quote in the second paragraph of the lesson: *"The circumstances of your life are not a comment on what God thinks about you. The cross is God's statement of how much He loves you and how determined He is to care for you."* Ask the group: "Do you agree with that statement? Why or why not?"

Ask someone to read Philippians 4:10–13, 19. Ask, "Which statements in this passage reinforce God's care and provision for His children?"

Write the word *SOVEREIGN* on the board vertically. Ask members for words that describe God, beginning with each letter. Some possibilities:

S	=	*supreme, superior*
O	=	*overall, omnipotent*
V	=	*virtuous, valuable, valiant, victorious*
E	=	*eternal, exalted*
R	=	*ruler, Redeemer, righteous*
E	=	*everlasting, endless*
I	=	*immutable, indefatigable*
G	=	*good, gracious*
N	=	*near, never-failing*

Discuss as a group things God has redeemed. Mention specific life experiences that have been redeemed by God such as physical pain/well-being, inner turmoil/peace, grief/comfort, confusion/ clarity, sin/forgiveness, disappointment/contentment, etc. Compare God's exchanges to exchanges in a store. For example, God puts no limitations on who He will redeem. He redeems all.

Ask members to share personal testimonies of God's redemptive power in their lives. Mention the redemption of the prisoners who are now in seminary preparing for ministry. Encourage group members to share how God redeemed them or others they know.

Closing (5 minutes)
Close with sentence prayers thanking God for recognizing, ruling over, and redeeming our life circumstances.

Prayer Time (5 minutes)
Guide members to use the acrostic JOY as they pray. Suggest they spend time praising JESUS for who He is, praying for the specific needs of OTHERS, and praying particularly for YOURSELF.

Review (5 minutes)
Ask the group members to share challenging circumstances that have occurred this week. Remind them that God still recognizes, rules over, and redeems our circumstances. Challenge members to be content in *all* circumstances.

Digesting Contents for Contentment (5 minutes)
Invite group members read Luke 3:8–14, noting particularly verse 14. Urge members to silently ask God, "What am I to do regarding my life's work?" Intimidating or accusing falsely are dishonest methods of getting ahead. Ask members to brainstorm other workplace strategies Christians should avoid. Discuss being content with your wages. Note that wages may not always be monetary recompense but may include intangibles such as praise, satisfaction with a job well done, ministry to others, etc.

Group Discussion (40 minutes)
Refer group members to the four statements about work in the Bible study. Ask, "Do you agree or disagree with these statements?" Urge members to suggest Scriptures that support their ideas.

Ask individuals or small groups to read these three passages: Ecclesiastes 2:17–26; Ecclesiastes 4:4–8; Ecclesiastes 5:10–20. Ask groups to summarize the specific teachings about work.

Ask each member to describe her life's work and estimate how long she has been doing it. Total the number of years of work represented in the group combined. Ask, "Have you been content in your work?"

Read Ecclesiastes 4:5–8 chorally as a reminder that life and work are useless if they are lived for one's own gain.

Teacher:	The fool folds his hands and consumes his own flesh.
Group:	**Vanity of vanities, all is vanity.**
Teacher:	Better a handful with quietness than both hands full, together with toil and grasping for the wind.
Group:	**Vanity of vanities, all is vanity.**
Teacher:	Yet there is no end to his labors, nor is his eye satisfied with riches.
Group:	**Vanity of vanities, all is vanity.**
Teacher:	But he never asks, "For whom do I toil and deprive myself of good?" This also is vanity and a grave misfortune.
Group:	**Vanity of vanities, all is vanity.**

Review Jesus' parable in Luke 12:13–21. Ask members to share the parables they wrote. If they did not do the activity, allow time for it now.

Closing (5 minutes)
Read aloud the quote by St. Augustine. Remind the group to love God more than work. Lead in a closing prayer expressing that commitment.

Prayer Time (5 minutes)
As members come in, ask them to find Matthew 6:8–13 in their Bibles and meditate on Jesus' model prayer. Say, "Let God fill you with peace and contentment as you think on these things."

Review (5 minutes)
Reflect on the teachings about work from the book of Ecclesiastes. Ask group members to suggest other biblical teachings about work.

Digesting Contents for Contentment (5 minutes)
Read this week's "Contents for Contentment" verse together. This verse expresses the Israelites' discontentment with the results of following God's plan to cross the Jordan. Let group members silently paraphrase the verse, substituting areas in their own lives in which they are discontent with the way God's plan is going. For example, *"Oh that I had been content single, and never married"* Or *"Oh that I had been content in my last job, and never left it for this one."*

Next, lead a time of silent prayer, of self examination, of confession, and of petition: "Lord, forgive my discontentment. Oh, that I would be content with (your will for my life)." After the prayer, ask volunteers to tell their areas of discontent.

Group Discussion (40 minutes)

Review with the group the list of *dis-* words. Describe how these negative feelings and emotions affect contentment.

Write these words on the board: *sin, surroundings, selfishness.* Call for three different people to each read one of the following Scriptures: *Psalm 51:10; Matthew 22:37–39; 1 John 2:15.* Discuss the way God wants people to handle these sources of discontentment.

Allow time for group members to answer for themselves the questions from the book *When is Enough, Enough?* Encourage women to recognize signs of discontent and begin removing them with the help of the Holy Spirit.

Read 3 John 1–14. Ask the group to describe the three men mentioned by John: Gaius, Diotrephes, and Demetrius. Ask them to decide whether each man seemed to be content or discontent.

Ask members of the group to share some of the commandments for contentment rom Customize Contentment.

Urge members to work together choosing ten commandments that would be helpful for the entire group.

Closing (5 minutes)

Give several different group members note cards with one of the following prayer topics: marriage, family, work, church, circumstances. Ask those holding cards to pray specifically for God to protect from discontentment in the areas printed on the cards they hold.

Prayer Time (5 minutes)

Pray these Scriptures. Ask different members to read these verses as prayers: *Romans 1:8; 1 Corinthians 1:10; 2 Corinthians 1:3–4; Galatians 1:3; and Ephesians 1:3–6.*

Review (5 minutes)

Review last week's discussion about the effects of sin, surroundings, and selfishness on Christians. Ask, "How can we handle these challenges and avoid discontentment?"

LESSON TEN

Digesting Contents for Contentment (5 minutes)

Invite a group member to read aloud Philippians 3:13–14. Ask group members what believers are to forget and what believers are to reach forward to. Suggest members silently search verses 8–14 for the goal we are pressing toward. Ask volunteers to share insights with the group.

Group Discussion (40 minutes)

Explain the tenses of salvation. Ask group members to define *justification* based on their personal study.

Ask three volunteers to read the following Scriptures: *Psalm 103:12; Jeremiah 31:34; 1 John 1:9.* Guide the group in contrasting God's forgiveness and our forgiveness.

God's Forgiveness	Our Forgiveness
complete	incomplete
everlasting	temporary
available	conditional

Pose this question, "How do you forgive others?" Ask members to answer honestly though they do not have to share personal details aloud. Suggest they determine how God would want them to forgive others.

Discuss times when group members have doubted or questioned God. Ask, "How did those doubts affect your faith?" Read Psalm 73:28 as a reminder of the faith believers must have in God.

Provide hymnals or song sheets with the words of "Trust and Obey." Lead the group in singing the song as a commitment.

Closing (5 minutes)

Give each member a blank note card. Direct members to each write on a card a sin of the past. These personal confessions are not to be shared with others. Remind the group of the forgiveness of God. Encourage women to tear the cards and throw them in the trash as a symbol of God's complete and total forgiveness of past sin. Close in a prayer of thanksgiving for God's grace and forgiveness.

Prayer Time (5 minutes)

Use this model for the prayer time as women voice sentence prayers aloud:

> A = adoration
> C = confession
> T = thanksgiving
> S = supplication

LESSON ELEVEN

Review (5 minutes)

Remind group members of God's promise to forgive past sin. Ask women if they have let go of the sin they gave to God during the closing commitment of the last meeting. If so, they should feel greater contentment.

Digesting Contents for Contentment (5 minutes)

Read aloud Jeremiah 29:11. Invite group members with different Bible translations to read the verse aloud. Ask the women to think back on times they traveled with their families or with a group. Ask if groups had one person in the group who did all the planning while everyone else followed along. Pose the question, "How important is it to you to *know* the plan?" Point out the first phrase in Jeremiah 29:11 and note that God knows the plans He has for us. Ask group members to identify what those plans are like. *(For welfare, not for calamity, and to give hope or other words from other translations or versions).* Express thanksgiving to each other for God as the ultimate vacation—and life—planner!

Group Discussion (40 minutes)

Review the tenses of salvation with the group. Ask women to develop a working definition for *sanctification.*

Ask group members to read the following passages: *Exodus 3:1–4; Exodus 19:3–6; 1 Kings 19:12–13; Isaiah 6:1–8; Acts 9:1–9.* Identify both the person in the passage and how he experienced God's presence. Encourage group members to share times they greatly felt God's presence.

Direct the group to find Jeremiah 29:11–13 in their Bibles. Suggest members read the passage silently and underline key words and phrases. Ask them to meditate on the promise of God's plan for them. Pose the question, "How do you know God's plan for your life?"

Psalm 91 provides visual pictures of the protective care of God. After you read the psalm for the group, ask group members to visualize with words or pictures God's protection (i.e. shadow, refuge, fortress, wings.) Recall together times God has covered you with His care.

Closing (5 minutes)

Close in prayer by asking members to read the following benedictions by the apostle Paul: Philippians 4:19–20; Colossians 4:2–6; 1 Thessalonians 5:23–28; 2 Thessalonians 3:16–18; 1 Timothy 6:20–21; and 2 Timothy 4:17–18.

Prayer Time (5 minutes)

Open with prayer thanking God for His future plans for you. Praise Him for the hope that believers have. Pray silently, allowing members to pray for those who do not have the hope of glorification.

Review (5 minutes)

Ask members if their definitions of contentment have changed in the course of the study. Make changes to your group definition that are agreed upon by group members. Ask members to share one insight on contentment that has been meaningful to them in this study.

Digesting Contents for Contentment (5 minutes)

Brainstorm mysteries about the faith that often baffle Christians. Ask women to find 2 Corinthians 4:18 in their Bibles and read it aloud together. Ask members what, according to the verse, believers are to look at. Suggest members meditate a few moments on the verse. List things that are *seen* or *temporal* and things that are *not seen* or *eternal*.

Group Discussion (40 minutes)

Review the tenses of salvation. Ask members to define glorification based on their study this week.

Discuss the difference between *concern* for the future and *fear* of the future. Ask group members what future things people commonly fear. List women's responses on the board. Ask members to identify things on the list over which God is sovereign. Erase each one as it is mentioned. You will, of course, erase everything. Ask members what Christians have to fear. The answer is "nothing."

Read aloud the four passages in John (John 3:15–16; 3:36; 10:28; 17:3). Discuss the group's understanding of eternal life. Pose the question, "What hope does eternal life give you for the future?"

Closing (5 minutes)

Conclude by asking members to write a personal commitment to share God's message of contentment with others. Distribute envelopes for members to address to themselves. Ask them to place their letters in the envelopes. Mail the letters one month after the study as a reminder of their commitments.

BIBLIOGRAPHY

Adels, Jill Haak. *The Wisdom of the Saints: An Anthology.*
   (New York: Oxford University Press, 1987).

Ashner, Laurie and Mitch Meyerson. *When Is Enough Enough?*
   (Center City, MI: Hazelden, 1996).

Briscoe, Jill. "Flying Through Fear."
   (Virtue, March/April 1994, p. 68).

Butler, Trent C. *Holman Bible Dictionary.*
   (Nashville: Holman Bible Publishers, 1991).

Foster, Richard J. *Celebration of Discipline: The Path to Spiritual Growth.*
   (New York: Harper & Row, 1988).

Jeffress, Robert. *The Road Most Traveled: Releasing the Power of Contentment in Your Life.*
   (Nashville: Broadman & Holman, 1996).

Kushner, Harold. *When All You've Ever Wanted Is Not Enough.*
   (New York: Pocket Books, 1986).

Peck, M. Scott. *The Road Less Traveled.*
   (New York: Touchstone, 1978).

Piper, John. *The Legacy of Sovereign Joy.*
   (Wheaton: Crossway Books, 2000).

Powell, John. *Happiness Is an Inside Job.*
   (Valencia, CA: Tabor Publishing, 1989).

Prager, Dennis. *Happiness Is a Serious Problem.*
   (New York: Regan Books, 1998).

Prather, Hugh. *Notes on How to Live in the World and Still Be Happy.*
   (New York: Doubleday, 1986).

Retton, Mary Lou. *Gateways to Happiness.*
   (New York: Broadway Books, 2000).

Roberts, Patti and Sherry Andrews. *Ashes to Gold*.
 (Nashville: Word, 1985).

Rowland, Michael D. Absolute Happiness: *The Way to a Life of Complete Fulfillment*.
 (Carlsbad, CA: Hay House, 1995).

Sala, Harold J. *Joyfully Single in a Couples' World*.
 (Camp Hill, PA: Horizon Books, 1998).

Smith, Hannah Whitall. *The Christian's Secret of a Happy Life*.
 (Westwood, NJ: Barbour & Co, 1985, first published in 1870).

Stephens, Kenneth H. *The Sacred Path to Contentment*
 (Nashville: Broadman & Holman, 1998).

Thayer, Joseph Henry. *Thayer's Greek-English Lexicon*.
 (Grand Rapids: Zondervan, 1970).

Wagner, C. Peter. *How Your Spiritual Gifts Can Help Your Church Grow*.
 (Ventura, CA: Regal Books, 1979).

Warren, Neil Clark. *Finding Contentment: When Momentary Happiness Just Isn't Enough*.
 (Nashville: Thomas Nelson, 1997).

Watson, Thomas. *The Art of Divine Contentment*.
 (Morgan, PA: Soli Deo Gloria Publications, 1995, first published in 1653).

Wiersbe, Warren W. *Be Satisfied: Looking for the Answer to the Meaning of Life*.
 (Colorado Springs: Victor Books, 1990).

The Woman's Study Bible.
 (Nashville: Thomas Nelson, 1995).

Yohn, Rick. *Discover Your Spiritual Gift and Use It*.
 (Wheaton: Tyndale House, 1974).

Also in the Woman's Guide series, these Bible studies by Rhonda H. Kelley challenge women to deeper levels of spiritual health and holiness.

1-56309-434-7

Using the examples of servant leaders throughout the Bible and especially the master example of Jesus, this study illuminates the most powerful practice of great leaders—servanthood.

1-56309-432-0

Concise but thorough, this topical workbook study contains 12 weekly lessons to challenge women to lead a Christlike lifestyle. Teaching guide included.

1-56309-252-2

This workbook study guide of 12 weekly lessons based on Colossians reminds readers not to wait until there's a problem to monitor their spiritual health. Teaching guide included.

You will find penetrating challenges from Scripture and helpful tools for thoughtful introspection.

—Dorothy Patterson, Assistant Professor of Women's Studies, Southeastern Baptist Theological Seminary

If you desire to exhibit peace and joy, you must strive for a holy life. [A Woman's Guide to Personal Holiness] *will change your concept of holiness—and your life.*

—Karen J. Hayter, Ed. D., Producer, Broadcast Communications Center, SBC

As soon as I picked up A Woman's Guide to Personal Holiness, *I could not put it down! Rhonda gives us a wonderful tool for every woman to be able to apply holiness to her life.*

—Jaye Martin, HeartCall Women's Evangelism, North American Mission Board

---

Available in Christian bookstores everywhere.

New Hope Publishers

Equipping You to Share the Hope of Christ